A Teacher's Guide to Managing ADHD in the Classroom

Teaching Success from Kindergarten to High School

Richard Bass

Table of Contents

Introduction

Sometimes I've got too many thoughts at once. It's like there's a four-way intersection in my brain where everyone's trying to go at the same time.
–A. J. Finn

Students With ADHD Are More Common Than You Think

Research shows that 6 million US children (close to 10% of the child population), aged 3-17, were diagnosed with attention-deficit hyperactivity disorder (ADHD) between 2016 and 2019 (Centers for Disease Control and Prevention, 2022). Many of them were boys, and typically diagnosed during elementary school.

Despite the prevalence of ADHD in children, the classroom environment may not always be accommodating to their needs. One of the reasons for this is that ADHD symptoms look similar to emotional and behavioral problems. From an educator's perspective, hyperactive symptoms of ADHD such as fidgeting, not following directions, or blurting out answers in class can be passed as difficult student behavior. The teacher may assume the child is attempting to disrupt the class or challenge their authority.

On the other hand, students with the inattentive type of ADHD are at a worse disadvantage because their symptoms are almost invisible. These quiet students get distracted easily and have trouble completing tasks on time or staying organized. They tend to fly under the radar or come across as lazy or careless.

With almost 10% of children diagnosed with ADHD, and many more who have not yet received diagnoses, there is no doubt that ADHD is prevalent in the classroom. The challenge that many teachers face is recognizing the signs of ADHD and adjusting their teaching styles to accommodate students who may be having trouble concentrating, regulating their emotions and behaviors, and engaging with their peers.

Why Does This Book Matter?

ADHD symptoms can change or become progressively worse over time as students age. A student who started out showing signs of hyperactivity may gradually show signs of inattentiveness, like having trouble focusing, following through with tasks, and staying organized. The progression of symptoms can impact students' academic performance and relationships with teachers and classmates. Due to being disruptive in class, talking too much, or not reading social cues, they may find themselves in unpleasant situations.

Teachers are important in helping students achieve their academic goals and feel supported in their learning. They have the enormous responsibility of setting up a classroom environment that is inclusive, nurturing, and conducive to learning. Whether students are neurotypical or neurodivergent, teachers are challenged to bring out the best in every child. The purpose of this comprehensive guide is to provide valuable insights and practical tools to help teachers enhance their ability to support students with ADHD and create inclusive learning environments.

Who Is This Book For?

The content of this book will be helpful for teachers across various demographics, who instruct students from kindergarten through high school level. What draws teachers to this book is their interest in gaining practical knowledge and strategies to effectively support students with ADHD in the classrooms. They seek guidance on understanding ADHD, recognizing its symptoms, and making students with ADHD feel accommodated and motivated to learn.

Both novice and experienced teachers, ranging from recent graduates to seasoned educators with years of classroom experience will walk away with valuable information that can enhance their existing classroom approaches. The book covers a wide range of topics about ADHD, including foundational knowledge and advanced practical techniques to address ADHD-related challenges.

The Journey Ahead

Since there is a lot of information to cover, the book has been divided into four parts. Each part focuses on a specific theme related to ADHD in the classroom. The four parts are as follows:

- **Part 1:** Understanding ADHD and Your Role as an Educator

- **Part 2:** Managing ADHD Behaviors

- **Part 3:** ADHD-Friendly Communication in the Classroom

- **Part 4:** Creating a Supportive Classroom Environment for Students With ADHD

The first part provides an introduction to ADHD and shares knowledge about what ADHD is and how it is diagnosed. The second part identifies the symptoms and behavioral-learning challenges that students who live with this condition may display. The third part takes a practical approach and teaches various creative and evidence-based strategies to make learning fun and engaging for students with ADHD. It also explores effective disciplinary measures that work. The fourth and final part discusses ways to create an inclusive and supportive classroom environment where students with ADHD feel accommodated and given enough resources and teaching aids to succeed.

This all-encompassing resource comes with practical exercises to support teachers in running a successful classroom. Each chapter ends with two interactive activities: one that teachers can complete alone and another that they can complete in a group setting with other educators. The goal is to provide opportunities to engage with the book material and practice the skills and strategies as the learning progresses.

With the knowledge and confidence gained from reading this book, teachers will feel prepared to address ADHD-related challenges in the classroom and create a classroom environment where all students can thrive!

PART 1:

Understanding ADHD and Your Role as an Educator

Chapter 1:

Demystifying ADHD

Behavior isn't something someone has. Rather, it emerges from the interaction of a person's biology, past experiences, and immediate context.
–L. Todd Rose

The Science Behind ADHD

ADHD is a neurological disorder that causes learning and behavioral problems, and over half of those who are diagnosed with ADHD have at least one other mental, emotional, or behavioral disorder, such as anxiety disorder, depression, autism spectrum disorder, or Tourette syndrome (Centers for Disease Control and Prevention, 2022b).

The good news is that 3 out of 4 (77%) children diagnosed with ADHD are receiving the proper treatment; they opt for ADHD medication (30%), behavioral therapy (15%), or a combination of both (32%) as preferred treatment options (Centers for Disease Control and Prevention, 2022b). There are however 23% of children diagnosed with ADHD who are not receiving any form of treatment, and an unknown percentage of children who despite displaying signs of ADHD, have not received medical diagnoses.

What does this mean for you as an educator? Your classroom consists of a diverse pool of students who have diverse needs. Some neurotypical students display what is considered normal neurological behaviors, but then there is a percentage of students who are neurodivergent and display atypical neurological behaviors. Some parents of neurodivergent students will inform you about their children's learning and developmental conditions, but not all parents will provide this information, mostly because they are unaware that their children are living with these conditions.

Even though you are a school teacher and not a doctor, it becomes extremely important for you to learn how to identify ADHD in students, so you can provide the support they need. Your support can also extend to parents who may be confused and even overwhelmed about their children's behaviors.

From a scientific standpoint, what you need to know about ADHD is that it is a condition that affects the size, structure, and function of the brain. Research shows that the brains of people with ADHD are smaller in size, particularly in the frontal lobe where executive functioning tasks like problem-solving, planning, impulse control, and emotional regulation are managed (WebMD, n.d.).

ADHD also slows brain development, which impacts cognitive tasks like paying attention, memorizing information, and staying focused. Eventually, brain development does catch up to that of people with normal brains, although it lags several years. An imaging study conducted by researchers at the National Institute of Mental Health found that the brain maturity of young people with ADHD was delayed by three years (National Institutes of Health, 2007). However, this delay didn't affect all regions of the brain. It was mostly evident in the frontal regions of the brain that controlled thinking, planning, and coordinating tasks.

In practical terms, this means that a 6-year-old student with ADHD has the brain development of a 3-year-old, and a 12-year-old student with ADHD has the brain development of a 9-year-old. Knowing this can shed light on why students with ADHD tend to act immature for their age or struggle with tasks that require memory, attention, and learning.

ADHD Characteristics

When you think of ADHD, you might picture students who can't sit still in class. Hyperactivity is one of the most recognizable symptoms of ADHD, but other silent symptoms of ADHD tend to go unnoticed. The acronym ADHD stands for attention-deficit hyperactivity disorder. From this medical term, two main characteristics of ADHD emerge: inattention and hyperactivity.

Other classroom-related behaviors they may have include:

- missing steps or details
- making careless mistakes

- forgetting instructions

- poor time management

- difficulty completing tasks on time

- losing focus while busy with tasks

- avoiding tasks that require mental focus

- difficulty keeping the workspace clean and tidy

- appearing dazed when being spoken to

About 25% of children with ADHD will be classified under *predominantly inattentive presentation* (Nichols, 2023). This small percentage is because symptoms of inattention go unnoticed many times. After all, they aren't as disruptive as hyperactivity. The majority of children with ADHD will be classified under *predominantly hyperactive presentation* and will exhibit the following classroom behaviors:

- fidgeting on the seat

- looking visibly restless

- talking excessively in class

- getting bored with tasks quickly

- difficulty sharing or waiting for their turn

- humming, singing, or making noises while playing

- blurting out answers or interrupting others without waiting for their turn

- running, jumping, or climbing during inappropriate times

- abruptly leaving their seat when they are expected to stay seated

Children who are suspected of having ADHD are first seen by a healthcare provider who will assess their symptoms and see whether they fit with the diagnostic criteria outlined in the American Psychiatric Association's Diagnostic and Statistical Manual, Fifth edition (DSM-5) (Centers for Disease Control and Prevention, 2022a). The diagnosis, however, is not made by the healthcare provider. They will refer children to mental health specialists like psychologists or psychiatrists, who will conduct further assessments and provide the next steps.

The DSM-5 criteria for inattention and hyperactivity are based on the symptoms listed above. For children up to the age of 16 to be diagnosed with inattention-type ADHD, they must display six or more inattention symptoms (children 17 years and old need to display five), for at least six months. Alternatively, for children up to the age of 16 to be diagnosed with hyperactive-type ADHD, they must display six or more hyperactivity symptoms (children 17 years and older need to display five), for at least six months.

Mental health specialists will also check whether the symptoms displayed are typical or atypical of the children's developmental level. Remember that ADHD affects brain development in certain areas, which means that children with ADHD will experience delays in picking up some cognitive and emotional skills. Other considerations that doctors will make before diagnosing children are:

- Determining whether several of the ADHD symptoms were present before reaching the age of 12.

- Determining whether ADHD symptoms are triggered in more than one social setting (e.g. at home, school, friend's house, while playing sports, etc.)

- Seeking to understand how the prevalence of ADHD symptoms affects children's everyday activities and routines.

- Assessing whether there might be any underlying conditions or co-occurring conditions that have similar symptoms.

It is also possible for children to display a combination of inattention and hyperactive symptoms. The diagnostic process would be the same, except they would need to exhibit enough symptoms of both characteristics for at least six months. Since ADHD symptoms can evolve, it is common for children to start out showing predominantly inattentive or hyperactive symptoms but then gradually display both. When the presentation of ADHD changes, a new diagnosis and treatment plan will be required.

There is no known cure for ADHD, but various treatment options are available for managing symptoms. Doctors will recommend prescription medications to improve focus, reduce hyperactivity, and regulate moods. They will also advise children to start psychotherapy to develop coping skills, overcome negative thoughts and emotions, and learn positive ways to relate to others. Psychotherapy is recommended to parents of children with ADHD as well, to help them learn effective stress management techniques, positive parenting skills, and receive emotional support.

Causes of ADHD in Children

The exact cause of ADHD hasn't been discovered. However, doctors have speculated on what makes some children more vulnerable to ADHD than others. Three factors that make a huge impact are genetics, brain structure, and environment. ADHD can be inherited from parents, siblings, or other family members who have previously been diagnosed with the condition. Researchers are still investigating just how ADHD is inherited because there isn't a specific genetic fault that is linked to ADHD.

Moreover, children with different brain structures, such as certain areas of the brain being smaller or larger than usual, are vulnerable to ADHD. These changes to brain structure can lead to impairments of some brain functions (i.e. executive function tasks) or an imbalance in the levels of brain chemicals produced.

Lastly, the environment inside the womb as well as the environment that children are born into can increase the risk of ADHD. Researchers have found that severe maternal stress during pregnancy can lead to infants developing ADHD symptoms after birth (Grizenko et al., 2012). Other factors that contributed to this were smoking, drug use, and consuming alcohol during pregnancy. ADHD is also believed to be connected to premature delivery (being born before the 37th week of pregnancy), low birth weight, epilepsy, or brain injuries inside the womb or early in life.

Parental styles and family dynamics are psychosocial factors that can make children vulnerable to ADHD during the first few years of life, the critical stages of cognitive development. How parents and family members interact with children and respond to their physical and emotional needs can cause behavioral and developmental problems. In particular, childhood emotional neglect and overly authoritarian parenting (i.e. being strict and enforcing harsh discipline) trigger chronic stress and anxiety in children, which negatively impacts their brain development.

The Impact of ADHD on Learning

Many children start school before their ADHD symptoms have developed to the extent of causing alarm. There may be some students in your classroom who show signs of ADHD that haven't been detected by their parents. Educators are sometimes the first to bring these symptoms to parents' attention and kickstart the process of getting diagnosed.

Early detection and treatment of ADHD can significantly improve students' academic performance and social life at school. Without the proper medical interventions, students with ADHD can fall behind in school, receive more negative feedback from teachers than neurotypical students (due to some disruptive symptoms), and feel socially alienated from their peers. Your understanding of the condition and how it presents itself in the classroom can make a positive impact on students' educational careers.

The good news is that schools can assist students with ADHD to cope with their learning environments. They may qualify for special education services that include one-on-one or group classes with a special education teacher or special accommodations in the classroom, such as modifications to how tasks, assignments, and tests are designed and administered. Classroom teachers may also track and write up progress reports on students' behaviors and recommend further assessments or services if they require concern.

Moreover, students with ADHD tend to struggle with stress and unexpected change. With recent changes in how school is conducted, brought on by the COVID-19 pandemic, some students may find it difficult to adjust to virtual learning. Fortunately, special education services can be used by schools that have incorporated distance learning. However, with fewer classes to attend, a less structured approach to learning, and social isolation from peers, getting accustomed to virtual learning can present unique challenges for students with ADHD.

However, with that said, not all students with ADHD will react the same to their learning environments. This is why tailoring support for each student is necessary. More than that, the involvement and support from parents can help you understand students' needs better and establish a meaningful plan for them.

Group Activity: Brainstorming Session

Sit around with other teachers and brainstorm the common misconceptions about ADHD. Afterward, discuss and debunk these misconceptions based on your professional experiences and the knowledge you have gained from reading this chapter.

Individual Activity: Self-Reflection

Reflect on your understanding of ADHD before reading this chapter and compare it to what you have learned. More particularly, consider how you viewed students with ADHD before learning about how their condition manifests. Recall moments when you mistakenly confused ADHD symptoms with acts of defiance.

This chapter has taught you the science behind ADHD and how the condition impacts students' learning and classroom behaviors. The next chapter looks closely at ADHD-related behaviors and provides systematic observation and assessment techniques to help you identify students with ADHD.

Chapter 2:

Differentiating ADHD From Typical Student Behavior

For reasons we don't quite understand, soon after you command yourself to pay attention, you forget that you commanded yourself to pay attention.
–Edward M. Hallowell

The Spectrum of Student Behavior

Just as there is a variety of fish in the sea, there are various types of students in the classroom. Having an understanding and appreciation of the diverse students in your classroom prepares you for unexpected situations and enables you to create a comfortable space where everyone feels included. Learning about different student behaviors can also help you distinguish between ADHD and non-ADHD symptoms and take the most appropriate course of action!

Here are common types of students that you will find in a classroom:

Teachers Pets

The teacher's pet is a driven student who positions themselves at the center of the teacher's attention. They will often pick a seat close to the teacher's desk or in the front of the classroom so they can focus in class. To show their dedication, they will ask questions, work quietly, hand in assignments on time, and seek to get to know the teacher better.

High Achievers

The high achiever is a diligent student who ranks among the top in their class for academic performance. They tend to possess a Type A personality, which makes them competitive, organized, ambitious, and perfectionists. Outside of the classroom, they may participate in social clubs and other extracurricular activities. They function on overdrive and are comfortable working independently.

Class Clowns

The class clown is a sociable student, who loves entertaining their peers. They use their sense of humor to make light of classroom situations and distract themselves from boredom. Even though a class clown makes jokes frequently, they tend to have natural intelligence. Sometimes, being naturally smart causes them not to apply themselves to learning. What they seem to enjoy the most is networking and building strong bonds with their peers.

Carefree and Clueless

The carefree and clueless student looks dazed and confused in any classroom situation. It can be difficult for a teacher to tell what the student is thinking or whether they are following and understanding instructions. They show signs of being distracted, such as looking outside the window, being lost in their thoughts, and asking questions that have already been answered.

Creative Geniuses

The creative genius is a student who lives in their creative bubble. They don't have a lot of friends in the classroom, but they have enough creative juices flowing in their mind to keep them busy. The creative genius performs well when engaging in creative tasks like writing, drawing, brainstorming ideas, and planning projects. Some of them are fascinated with specific subjects or topics and may show disinterest in others.

It is also normal for students to behave badly in the classroom. Remember that your students come from different social and cultural backgrounds and what is deemed acceptable in their homes or communities could be considered inappropriate in the classroom. Examples of bad classroom etiquette include:

- lying
- stealing
- cheating
- back-talking

- cell phone usage

- arriving late to class

- sniping remarks

- side conversations

- disregarding deadlines

Students may also be immature, careless, or attention-seeking due to their developmental age. As frustrating as these troublesome behaviors may be, they are nothing to be concerned about, except when the behaviors don't match students' developmental age (i.e. a student in fourth grade behaving like they are in first grade), or when these behaviors persist after calling them out and implementing disciplinary measures.

Troublesome behaviors are not always a sign of ADHD. Other factors that might cause students to misbehave are ongoing health problems, family conflict or instability, adjusting to recent changes (e.g. transitioning from physical to distant learning), or general learning difficulties. If you have reasons to believe that much larger problems are at play, you can call your students aside and speak to them or their parents.

Identifying ADHD-Related Behaviors

How can you distinguish between normal troublesome behaviors and ADHD symptoms in the classroom? This is a question that many educators ask themselves. The truth is that ADHD can be confused with defiance or resemble other mood, behavioral, and developmental disorders. It is only through observation and recording patterns that you can identify ADHD and refer struggling students to the relevant mental health professionals for further assessments.

In the previous chapter, we took an in-depth look at the three characteristics of ADHD, which are inattentiveness, hyperactivity, and a combination of both. Factors to consider when assessing your students' symptoms include:

Severe Impairments

High energy or lack of focus in the classroom are not always signs of ADHD. To be diagnosed with this condition, children need to display these symptoms for an extended period (i.e. at least six months) and there has to be evidence of their behaviors interfering with their performance, sociability, moods, and overall well-being.

Age and Gender

When analyzing students' symptoms, compare their classroom behaviors to children in the same developmental age. If they are 14 years old, compare their behaviors to other 14-year-old children. Be particularly vigilant for symptoms of ADHD among female students, as they commonly suffer from the inattentive type of ADHD, which is less disruptive and therefore less noticeable. Due to social conditioning, girls will attempt to *mask* their symptoms and seem as though they are doing fine. Some will compensate for their inattentiveness by chronically working, being perfectionists, or being hard on themselves when they fall behind or make mistakes.

Other Conditions

As mentioned above, ADHD symptoms can sometimes be signs of other conditions. For example, being dazed or distracted in class could be a sign of anxiety or depression. Perhaps there is an upcoming test that has gotten your student worried or stressful situations happening at home. Another example is an undiagnosed learning disorder like dyslexia or speech problems that can cause delays in reading, comprehension, and developing healthy social skills. Other conditions that have similar symptoms to ADHD include obsessive-compulsive disorder (OCD), post-traumatic stress disorder (PTSD), oppositional defiant disorder (ODD), and autistic spectrum disorder (ASD).

Keeping a constant eye on your students and documenting behaviors that are out of the norm can help you understand their symptoms better and offer additional learning and emotional support. It can also be useful to have open lines of communication with parents so that you feel comfortable discussing your students' behaviors with them and working together to find the best solutions.

Observation and Assessment Strategies

Response to Intervention (RTI) is an evidence-based practice that uses data to identify students with learning challenges or disabilities, monitor their progress, and provide suitable interventions (Haraway, 2012). This structured approach to understanding student behavior can help educators identify signs of ADHD, track the progression of symptoms over time, and take the necessary steps to provide at-risk students with professional support.

One of the core principles of RTI is that effective behavioral interventions must be carried out in levels, or tiers, beginning with classroom assessments and moving to more targeted interventions for students who display severe learning impairments. The RTI framework consists of three tiers for observing and managing student behaviors:

- **Tier 1:** General research-based assessments and behavioral strategies applicable to all students in the classroom.

- **Tier 2:** Smaller group interventions with targeted students to observe and assess behaviors. Progress monitoring strategies are included to keep track of behavioral changes.

- **Tier 3:** Intense assessments that are reserved for students who have not shown any progress despite having gone through Tier 1 and Tier 2 interventions. These students may be referred to specialists who can offer more intensive interventions.

Below is a collection of behavioral assessment tools falling under the three tiers that are appropriate to use in your classroom. Administer these assessment tools when identifying and monitoring ADHD symptoms. If there are students in your classroom displaying severe learning impairments or challenging behaviors, use individualized assessment tools. In most cases, there will be very few students who qualify for Tier 3 interventions.

Before administering these behavioral assessment tools, consider sitting down and having a conversation with the affected students' parents. Share your concerns and introduce the RTI framework. Explain how each of the assessment tools below works and how their children may benefit from them. Keep parents informed about their children's progress and any behavioral changes that occur.

Tier 1 and Tier 2: Behavioral Assessment Tools

For general classroom behavioral management and identifying challenging behaviors, you can conduct Tier 1 and Tier 2 behavioral assessments. The following tools will help you reinforce positive behaviors in the classroom and screen for ADHD symptoms.

Curriculum Based Measurement

There are certain academic skills that students need to acquire at each education level. For instance, based on the phase or grade, they may be required to learn reading, writing, comprehension, and mathematics skills. Curriculum Based Measurement (CBM) involves designing frequent assessments that cover a range of material taught in the classroom to evaluate students' skills in various subjects. You can design your own assessments and schedule them on a weekly or monthly basis. The outcomes of the assessments will be collected as data and used to measure students' progress.

Office Discipline

Most classroom misconduct can be handled by educators without taking additional measures like sending students to the principal's office. However, some behaviors disrupt lessons and pose a risk to teachers and other students. Examples of some of these behaviors include yelling at the teacher or fellow students, disrespecting the authority of the teacher, bullying fellow students, and acts of cheating, stealing, or vandalizing. These behaviors need to be identified and addressed before they get worse.

Sending students to the office not only helps you regulate student behaviors but can also help you identify students with behavioral issues. Keep a record of how many behavior incidents and disciplinary referrals each student has, as well as the outcomes of the referrals. When meeting with parents to discuss student behaviors, bring out the file with all of the behavior incidents and disciplinary referrals you noted during a certain period. If student behaviors do not improve, you may need to implement Tier 2 interventions which are more focused on addressing specific behavior issues in smaller groups.

School-Wide Information System

The school-wide information system (SWIS) is a web-based data collection and management software that was created at the University of Oregon during the 1990s (Haraway, 2012). The software was designed to enable schools to create records for all students across grades, or specific groups of students so that they can easily document and monitor behavioral and learning problems and provide targeted interventions. What makes this software effective for behavioral management is that it generates detailed reports that provide all of the information you need to know about a student's track record for misconduct.

Systematic Screening for Behavior Disorders

The systematic screening for behavior disorders (SSBD) is a two-step screening process for social skills and behavioral issues, designed for elementary school children. It consists of a standardized checklist system that includes rating scales for different behaviors. This tool can be administered to the entire class (i.e. Tier 1 intervention) or targeted students (i.e. Tier 2 intervention). You can also observe behaviors over a period and provide feedback on the progress of student behaviors.

Tier 2 and Tier 3: Behavioral Assessment Tools

There could be some students in your classroom that you suspect have ADHD or a similar condition. To further assess these students' behaviors, conduct Tier 2 and Tier 3 interventions in smaller groups or individual settings. Below are some effective behavioral assessment tools that you can implement.

Check-In Check-Out and Behavior Education Program

Once you have identified at-risk students, you will need to work with them individually or as a group and provide ongoing supervision. Check-in Check-out (CICO) and behavior education program (BEP) are two interventions that can help you do that. Both of them begin with setting behavioral goals and communicating behavior expectations. Students are then given clear instructions to follow and demonstrations to make sure they understand what is expected of them. Consequences for not following instructions (i.e. performing inappropriate behavior) are also explained and enforced when applicable.

Your job as the teacher is to monitor their progress and offer positive reinforcement regularly to keep students motivated. The involvement of parents is essential for the success of both interventions. While you can monitor behaviors in the classroom, parents are advised to monitor behaviors at home. Moreover, student monitoring cards are sent home periodically for parent acknowledgment and returned to school. The intensity of the interventions is adjusted or increased depending on the progress made. When students' behaviors have improved significantly, the interventions have faded out.

Direct Observation of Behavior

As the name suggests, direct observation of behavior involves analyzing the classroom behaviors of at-risk students and providing detailed notes of the tendency and frequency of performing certain behaviors. To make this intervention meaningful, be selective about the behaviors you are monitoring and choose to focus on one or two rather than a long list of behaviors.

Furthermore, decide how you will collect the data and at what times you are going to observe these behaviors. For example, will data be collected through class tests or by watching students in action? Will students be observed when they arrive in class, when they work in groups with other learners, when they begin assignments, or when you are standing in front of the class teaching? Your data should include a few important measurements, such as the frequency of the behavior (i.e. the number of times the behavior happens), the duration of the behavior (i.e. how long the behavior continues), and latency (i.e. how much time passes before the behavior starts again).

For comparison, you can observe the rate at which a student performs inappropriate behavior versus the rate at which they perform acceptable behavior. Make sure that you observe these behaviors using the same data collection method and within the same period. For example, you can observe how often a student blurts out an answer versus raising their hand or how long a student spends fidgeting versus sitting still while working. Lastly, to gain perspective on the targeted student's behaviors and compare them to the standard, it is recommended to observe another student's behaviors simultaneously. This extra step will help you determine whether the target student's behaviors are typical of classroom behaviors or evidence of a specific problem.

Self-Monitoring

The ultimate goal of behavioral interventions is to help students understand why certain behaviors are inappropriate in the classroom and encourage them to correct themselves whenever they behave improperly. Self-monitoring is a skill that can be incorporated into other behavioral interventions or set as the long-term goal. The aim is to teach at-risk students what inappropriate behaviors look like and how to counter them. The process begins by defining a targeted behavior (i.e. fidgeting) and then setting a goal. Thereafter, you can show students age-appropriate ways to counter the targeted behavior. Students can record progress on their own or when instructed by you. Visual charts and checklists are great ways to help students review their progress on a regular basis. Decide how often you would like to meet with students to discuss goals and provide feedback. Modify the program whenever necessary and negotiate suitable rewards for reaching milestones.

The best part about using the RTI framework to identify, monitor, and address ADHD behaviors in the classroom is that you get to develop a deeper bond with your students and provide meaningful support that can positively impact their educational careers. The framework encourages ongoing observations, supervision, and check-ins with students to ensure the interventions are producing the desired behavioral outcomes.

Group Activity: Student-Teacher Role-Play

Organize educators into pairs and give them a unique role-play scenario involving a student who displays ADHD behaviors and a teacher. Encourage them to act out the scenario in their respective roles and respond to the behaviors using the tools that were discussed in this chapter. The pairs can switch roles so that each person gets to play the role of the teacher.

Individual Activity: Behavior Observation

Look at the table below and identify behaviors that are typical of students with ADHD and those without ADHD. Confirm your responses by referring to Chapters 1 and 2 of the book.

difficulty staying focused on tasks	talking to peers during instruction time	constantly on the move and having trouble being still	difficulty following or remembering instructions
not completing homework assignments	impulsivity in speech and actions	arguing with peers	not paying attention due to boredom
difficulty waiting on their turn	asking a lot of questions	easily distracted by classroom stimuli	Staring out of the window
arriving late to class	talking excessively and blurting answers	having an attitude with the teacher	poor organizational skills
forgetfulness, including forgetting deadlines	being quiet during group work	fidgeting and squirming while seated	not socializing with peers

It can be difficult to distinguish between typical bad behavior and ADHD behaviors in the classroom. The fact is that students make poor choices sometimes and need to be corrected when they misbehave. However, when a pattern of inappropriate behaviors emerges that doesn't fit the student's developmental age, something more serious could be at play. Now that you have the tools to identify ADHD behaviors, we can proceed to the next chapter and discuss ways that you can support students with ADHD.

Chapter 3:

The Educator's Role in Supporting Students With ADHD

Most teachers and adults could benefit from pretending that all kids in their class have ADHD—what is good for kids with ADHD is good for all kids. –Edward M. Hallowell

Creating an Inclusive Learning Environment

A 2017 survey conducted by The ADHD Foundation found that half of the teachers polled had not received training to teach young students with ADHD (Robertshaw, 2023). This finding shows that unless teachers specialize in teaching students with special needs, many of them may not be informed about the various learning differences of neurodivergent students.

A common assumption that teachers make is to think what works for some students will work for every student. However, this isn't true, even among neurotypical students. Every student's brain is wired differently and how they absorb and process information may not be the same. Students diagnosed or showing symptoms of ADHD can keep up with the mainstream school curriculum without having to attend a special needs school. Nevertheless, their unique behavioral challenges can create additional obstacles when learning.

The solution to accommodating all students' learning styles is not to *dumb down* the content but instead to create an inclusive learning environment that caters to the diverse needs of your students. The word *inclusion* in the educational context means to accept every student regardless of their learning abilities or differences and create equal opportunities to thrive in the classroom. Being inclusive as a teacher is not about awarding students with ADHD certain privileges over the rest of the class. It is about creating a learning environment that works for all students, whether they have health conditions or not.

It is also worth noting that you don't need to change your learning material to create an inclusive learning environment. You simply need to be mindful of how you approach your lessons to ensure that no students are left scratching their heads and confused about how to engage with the material.

For example, delivering an oral presentation and writing keywords on a whiteboard could be the ideal learning style for some students in your classroom. However, there could be a handful who process information better when it is packaged as a video or illustrated on a chart or infographic. Still, there could be a select number of students who get bored and distracted when they are not actively participating in the lesson. They may stay engaged for longer when given Q&A sessions or short breakaway discussions.

As you can see, an inclusive learning environment is not only beneficial for students with ADHD but caters to the learning needs and preferences of all students. Every child is allowed to learn in a manner that suits them best, which creates a supportive and positive atmosphere in the classroom.

The fourth part of the book provides detailed strategies on how you can create an inclusive and supportive classroom environment for your students with ADHD. The strategies mentioned are applicable and beneficial for students without ADHD too. But for now, here are a few tips on how to create an inclusive learning environment:

- Define clear standards of behavior that apply to every student and enforce those standards regularly.

- Be sensitive in the way that you deal with minor disruptions or inconveniences in the classroom (e.g. student forgets their textbook at home).

- Provide all students with equal opportunities to speak. Identify students who have been quiet during discussions and offer them a chance to share their thoughts.

- Apply a scaffolded approach to learning where you guide students along and offer continued support until they grasp the concepts and can perform tasks independently.

- Get to know every student in your class and build friendly relationships. Ask them questions about their pets, hobbies, and friends to build friendly relationships.

- Find multiple ways to present learning materials to accommodate students' varied learning styles. The material should engage the five senses (i.e. sight, hearing, smell, taste, and touch).

- Assess students based on individual performance instead of classroom performance. Keep a record of students' progress and privately praise students who are doing well.

Collaborating With Parents and Professionals

Parents are necessary team players when seeking to understand and navigate ADHD-related challenges in the classroom. Many of them may not be knowledgeable about ADHD; however, they are familiar with their children's behaviors and can work with you to come up with the best learning approaches for them. When dealing with at-risk students, both you and their parents can monitor their behaviors at school and home and meet regularly to discuss progress. Parents can also review and sign a daily or weekly behavior report card to stay informed about their children's performance at school.

Some students in your classroom may be referred to special school services, mental health doctors, and therapists for additional assessments and support. Even though these interventions happen outside of your classroom, they have a significant impact on students' behavior and performance inside the classroom. Therefore, staying informed about your students' medical or therapeutic programs will allow you to monitor changes in the classroom and provide feedback to parents on any improvements or regressions.

The feedback loop between teachers, parents, and other professionals is important for sharing information about target students and collectively monitoring and analyzing behavioral patterns. It can also ensure that everyone is on the same page about the best treatments and interventions suitable for individual students.

Some of the ways that you can establish and nurture relationships with parents include:

Be Proactive

Communicate frequently with parents in a respectful and compassionate way. Update them on classroom activities by sending photos and videos and show that you care about the well-being of their children. Periodically, share student performance reviews or report cards with parents and provide a detailed summary of how their children are coping at school. If you have identified at-risk students, reach out to their parents and schedule a meeting or share classroom interventions that you have undertaken to offer additional support.

Be Approachable

Establish communication channels so that parents can reach you when they have questions or need to discuss concerns about their children. For example, in addition to email, you can create a private WhatsApp or Facebook group and invite all of the parents of students in your classroom. Share your contact details and convenient times when parents can contact you.

Share Strategies and Resources

Empowering parents to do more to support their children can make your job in the classroom much easier. Many parents are concerned about their children's behaviors but don't have the proper skills or training to manage their behaviors. Share evidence-based strategies and helpful resources that parents can use to manage their children's ADHD symptoms and support their learning at home.

For example, you can provide information related to improving students' time management, organizational skills, and concentration. You can also include information on age-appropriate stress management techniques, how to create a nurturing environment at home, and discipline strategies that work on children with ADHD. In addition to the resources you provide, create a curated list of reputable sources of information and relevant books, podcasts, or websites that parents can visit for more support.

Group Activity: Collaboration Simulation

Sit down with other educators and brainstorm different ways to collaborate with parents, doctors, counselors, and other professionals who play a supportive role in your students' lives. Share personal experiences and what has worked (or didn't work) for each of you in the past.

Individual Activity: Individualized Support Plan

Using the following template, create an individualized support plan for a fictional student with ADHD. Identify two behavioral concerns and create achievable objectives, interventions, and desired milestones. Fill out the template based on the information provided in Chapters 1, 2, and 3.

Student Name:	Year and Class:	Gender:	Date:	Review Date:
Behavior Concerns:	Objectives:	Interventions:	Desired Milestones:	Progress Notes:

Creating an inclusive learning environment ensures that all students are comfortable with the way that lessons are carried out and confident in their abilities to engage with the material. Involve parents, as much as possible, in students' learning to update them on the progress made and create an information-sharing feedback loop. The next chapter discusses the legal considerations that you need to make as an educator when supporting students with ADHD.

Chapter 4:

Legal and Ethical Considerations in ADHD Management

Never give up on someone with a mental illness. When "I" is replaced by "we," illness becomes wellness. –Shannon L. Alder

Understanding Legal Obligations

Every child has a right to access quality education. In the United States, the Department of Education ensures that all children have the opportunity to obtain skills and knowledge that will enable them to live successful lives. One of the arms of the Department of Education is the Office for Civil Rights (OCR). Its responsibility is to protect students with disabilities from discrimination on the basis of disability (US Department of Education, 2016).

On a daily basis, the OCR receives inquiries and complaints in the areas of elementary and secondary school education regarding educational services to students with disabilities, including those who have been diagnosed with ADHD. The OCR investigates cases of discrimination and mandates schools to offer special education services and reasonable accommodations for students who qualify for the programs.

Children who are eligible for special education services must fall under at least one of the categories below (NICHCY, 2011):

- autism
- deafness
- deaf-blindness
- hearing impairment
- emotional disturbance
- intellectual disability
- orthopedic impairment
- specific learning disability
- speech or language impairment
- traumatic brain injury
- visual impairment (including blindness)
- multiple disabilities

- other health impairment

Students with ADHD may fall under the "other health impairment," "emotional disturbance," or "intellectual disability" categories, depending on their diagnosis. However, there are some cases where students with ADHD do not qualify for special education services. For instance, when a student is capable of learning and continuing with their daily functioning without significant disturbances to their activities, they may not need these services. Students who show signs of ADHD but have not received a medical diagnosis may also be deemed ineligible to receive special education services.

Section 504 and IDEA

Two federal laws govern the funding and administration of special education services, as well as special accommodations for students with disabilities. These are Section 504 of the Rehabilitation Act of 1973 and the Individuals with Disabilities Education Act (IDEA) (US Department of Education, 2016). Please note that these laws apply to all state and local public school districts and private or independent schools that receive federal funding.

Section 504 is a federal law that protects students with disabilities and provides access to non-discriminatory services. According to the law, school districts must offer free and appropriate public education to students with disabilities, regardless of the type or severity of their disability (US Department of Education, 2016).

Moreover, school districts are required to provide student evaluations at no cost to parents or teachers, if they have reasons to believe that students have an undisclosed disability or would benefit from special education services. Parents can request evaluations when they suspect that their children may have ADHD or other unknown conditions affecting their learning. Parents are welcome to request evaluations even when they have already received a medical diagnosis from a doctor.

School districts can approve or reject requests for evaluations. However, they must explain their reasons for turning down requests and inform parents of the process to dispute the decision, outlined under Section 504. If a school district requires that a student start by getting a medical assessment to determine whether they have a disability or not, the costs of undergoing the assessment must be covered by the school district, at no charge to parents or teachers.

IDEA is a federal law that seeks to provide students with disabilities opportunities to develop their skills and knowledge, cultivate their gifts, and make a meaningful contribution to society. The law primarily focuses on assisting state and local public schools, educational service agencies, and federal agencies to offer comprehensive services to children with disabilities and their families. Emphasis is placed on improving the education curriculum, early childhood intervention services, transition planning, and accountability for ensuring the success of students with disabilities (U.S. Department of Education, 2023).

The type of support that students with ADHD will receive at school will depend on whether they meet the requirements for assistance outlined by these two federal laws. Students who qualify for special services will be evaluated and either receive Section 504 services included in a 504 Plan or an individualized education plan (IEP) that consists of special education services to meet their unique needs.

How Does the Referral Process Work?

As an educator, you play an important role in ensuring your students with ADHD get the additional support they deserve. The referral process starts with you having several discussions with the parents, doctors, or counselors of the affected student concerning their behaviors and possible interventions. During these discussions, collect as much data as you can on the student's academic and behavioral problems. The data can be collected through conversations with parents and students, observations in the classroom, and behavioral assessment tools.

At this stage, the student may or may not have received a medical diagnosis of ADHD. Do your best to encourage the parents to take their child for a medical assessment. Having a diagnosis creates a stronger case for seeking special educational services and can work to the student's advantage. Nevertheless, an ADHD diagnosis doesn't automatically guarantee a student will receive special education services. To qualify, their condition must have reached a critical stage where it starts to interfere with their learning at school.

Once you have gathered all of the necessary data to build a strong case, you can refer the student to the school district for an evaluation. If the evaluation request is approved, the student will undergo assessments from several professionals depending on their needs. A student with ADHD might be asked to visit a psychologist, pediatrician, neurologist, and social worker. The team of professionals will make observations, offer standardized tests, and compile a detailed evaluation report. The report will outline recommendations for the skills and services that the student will need.

Finally, a meeting will be scheduled with the team of professionals and the parents of the student to discuss the goals and intervention strategies of the comprehensive plan chosen (either the 504 Plan or the IEP Plan). You are welcome to join this meeting and offer suggestions on how you can support the student in the classroom environment.

Maintaining Privacy and Confidentiality

As an educator, you have access to a lot of student and family data due to the nature of your job. One of your many tasks is to keep a record of students' academic, medical, family, and disciplinary information. Handling this information with care is part of your ethical and legal obligation. The law mandates that you protect the privacy of your student's educational records to avoid lawsuits or financial penalties for your school.

Besides the legal implications, protecting your students' privacy and sensitive information allows you to build trusting relationships with them and their families. This can also have a positive impact on your reputation and reliability as an educator. When you are known to be an honest, trustworthy, and discrete teacher, students and parents can confide in you when facing personal or learning problems.

To safeguard your students' records, there are some safety measures that you can implement, such as:

Establish Clear Procedures

Your school has its policies on maintaining privacy and confidentiality. Find out what those policies are and what procedures you need to follow. If there aren't any specific policies established that deal with the handling of confidential information, create your own. Consider things like where you file or store the information, who has access to the information, how the information is shared, and for how long you keep the information. Share these confidentiality procedures with your student's parents and get their signed consent. Every year, review the procedures and make a few updates to provide added security.

Use Secure Storage Systems

Avoid using manual filing systems to store student records because they can lead to mishandling and loss of documents. They also present security issues when filing cabinets are left open or unsupervised or when documents are placed on your desk, left in the printing machine, or picked up by accident by someone else. Instead, use digital cloud-based storage systems that allow you to create password-protected databases. Popular choices include Dropbox, Google Drive, and OneDrive.

Limit Access to Information

Ideally, the private and confidential information that you keep on your students is not supposed to be shared with anybody. The information is collected and stored so that you can perform your duties to the best of your ability. However, there will be occasions when people request access to certain information about your students. These people could be their parents, other teachers, counselors, or doctors. You will need to decide when it is appropriate to share this information and with whom you can share the information. In general, if the information is required to assist the professional in fulfilling their tasks and responsibilities, then it is safe to share it with them (provided you have obtained content from the parents of the student). Share the information over secured channels and avoid using public or unsecured Wi-Fi networks.

Maintaining your students' privacy and confidentiality is your legal responsibility as a teacher. Learn about the different digital filing systems available that can help you make your job of safeguarding student educational records easier. Speak to other teachers and find out how they file their students' records.

Group Activity: Mock Evaluation Meeting

Sit on a table with a group of teachers and role-play a mock evaluation meeting for a student with ADHD. Decide on who is going to play the role of the parents and professional doctors. Center your discussions around the eligibility for special education services, goals and objectives for the IEP or 504 Plan, and specific accommodations that will need to be made for the student.

Individual Activity: Policy Review

Obtain a copy of your school's policy regarding the management of confidential information. Review the policy and summarize the procedures that you are obliged to follow as an educator. If you have any suggestions on how to improve the policy, write them down on a piece of paper and present them to the relevant stakeholders.

Students with disabilities have every right to access free and quality education, regardless of the type or severity of their disability. Provisions have been made by the US Department of Education to ensure students with ADHD receive additional educational support, if necessary. You can assist at-risk students by referring them to your school's district for evaluation.

We have now completed the first part of the book exploring the nature of ADHD and how it affects students in the classroom. Let us proceed to the second part of the book, which covers different classroom strategies for managing ADHD behaviors.

PART 2:

Managing ADHD-Related Behaviors

Chapter 5:

Classroom Strategies for Attention Difficulties

ADHD is real and valid. The sooner we recognize the patterns and learn to work with these kids, the better assured we will be that they as adults will be healthy members of society. —Rhonda Van Diest

Inattentiveness in the Classroom

Students with inattentive ADHD face unique challenges that impact their ability to pay attention and work diligently without being distracted. In kindergarten, inattentiveness can manifest as the inability to concentrate on tasks or conversations for longer than two minutes and difficulty managing transitions from one activity to another.

In elementary school, inattentiveness shows up as poor time management, the inability to start and complete assignments, or needing a lot of guidance and support to complete classwork. In middle and high school, inattentiveness manifests as frequent distractions and dazing out of the window, poor organizational skills and time-tracking, and difficulties memorizing notes and preparing for tests and exams.

In this chapter, we will look at different classroom strategies to support students who may have attention challenges. The strategies apply to students in general and are not specific to any grade.

Creating a Structured Environment

The first and perhaps most effective way of encouraging students to focus is to create a structured classroom. Students respond positively to structure because expectations are communicated, and this puts their minds at ease. Some students may come from homes where there is no structure or stability. When they enter your organized classroom and are expected to follow clear rules and instructions, their nervous systems calm down and they feel a sense of security, which improves their ability to absorb information.

A structured classroom environment translates to a safe and supportive environment. Students with attention challenges are likely to succeed in this type of environment because they are less anxious or confused about completing classwork. Building a structured environment starts with setting clear and positive boundaries that inform the type of interactions, discipline, and atmosphere you want to establish in your classroom. Consider the following boundaries that can enhance the structure of your classroom:

Create Classroom Standards

When students enter your classroom, they need to know how to relate to you and their peers, as well as the minimum standards expected of them. On the first day of school, the first day of the term, or even the first day of the new week, spend five minutes going over the classroom rules related to arriving on time, being quiet during instruction time, submitting homework assignments, and classroom etiquette. Possible consequences for breaking the rules should be discussed in depth so students understand the weight of their improper behaviors. Provide relatable scenarios of acceptable and unacceptable behaviors and be open to questions.

Set Daily and Weekly Goals

Students are motivated when they know that their work contributes to something bigger than themselves. To encourage consistent focus, start your day or week by setting small and realistic classwork goals. For example, reasonable goals could be to complete 10 math sums before the bell rings or to submit study notes for the upcoming test before the end of the week. The goals should be challenging while also inclusive of students' academic levels. Offer support to students who may be struggling or lagging. Encourage students to cheer for each other and see the achievement as a collective victory.

Hold Students Accountable for Their Actions

Students with ADHD are prone to low self-esteem due to living with learning and social disabilities that make them feel inadequate or self-conscious. The best thing that you can do as an educator is to believe in them and show them that they have the potential to thrive. Holding students accountable for their improper actions shows that you believe they can do better. Don't allow them to get comfortable with quitting, submitting incomplete work, throwing a tantrum when they are upset, or sulking when they don't get their way. Address these issues when they are still minor and haven't become habits. Enforce appropriate consequences and remind them that they can do better.

Promote Active Learning

Inattentiveness can make students appear dazed, distant, bored, or disinterested. As much as they want to focus on what you are saying, they get easily distracted by thoughts or external stimuli. To capture and hold their attention, you must make learning material engaging, otherwise, they might find something more exciting to look at or think about.

Active learning in the classroom refers to participating in lessons by taking action. Instead of standing in the front of the class and speaking to your students for 30 minutes while they listen and follow along, you invite them to get involved in the learning process. Students become collaborators in analyzing, sorting, and manipulating information, which allows them to brainstorm ideas, solve problems, and formulate meaningful insights about the information they are learning.

In an active learning environment, students are not given an opportunity to sit back and passively absorb information. Their brains are constantly switched on and working, even though it may not feel like it. Moreover, active learning allows students to network with each other and work as teams to understand and digest new information. For students who are academically behind, these group breakaway sessions can be encouraging.

How you choose to incorporate active learning into your lesson plans is completely up to you. Based on the content and learning objectives, you may have lessons that heavily rely on active learning and some lessons that don't. The type of strategies that you implement will also depend on what you hope to achieve with each lesson. Here is a list of active learning strategies that you can test on your students:

Polls and Quizzes

To assess how well your students understand the content, you can present a poll or quiz toward the end of the lesson. The questions should be based on information covered in class or homework that was recently completed. Have a classroom discussion about the questions before you reveal the correct answers. Allow students to re-vote (if it is a poll) or retake the quiz after the discussions.

Minute Paper

When introducing new concepts, ask your students to take out a sheet of paper and spend a minute writing down everything they know about the topic. Use a stopwatch to keep track of the time. After several lessons of teaching about the concept, ask them to take out the same piece of paper, turn it over, and spend another minute writing down everything they know about the topic. Before big tests or exams, you can carry out the same exercise. Encourage personal reflection on how much they have learned and the progress they have made.

Think—Pair—Present

Students are positively influenced by each other and can play an important role in offering academic support in the classroom. When you are teaching concepts that require advanced thinking skills and may seem confusing for some students, playing a game of think—pair—present can make the learning process less stressful. Start by asking students to think independently about a question for five minutes. Thereafter, get them to sit in pairs and share their thoughts for another five minutes. When the time is up, go around the room and ask each pair to stand up and present their answers. Write down all of the answers on the board so everyone can see them. Spend the rest of the lesson going through the answers and providing clarity.

Classroom Exit Tickets

You may not always know which students are actively listening and which ones aren't by simply looking at them. To make sure that everyone is on the same page and understands the content of the lesson, introduce classroom exit tickets. When students are preparing to pack up and leave the class, ask them to tear a small piece of paper (their exit ticket) and write down something new that they have learned and something they are still confused about. Students must remember to sign their tickets with their names. Collect the tickets as they walk out the door and use this as feedback to gauge the level of understanding and revisit certain concepts that students are struggling with in the next lesson.

Implementing Attention-Focusing Strategies

There is scientific evidence to explain why students with ADHD, particularly the inattentive type, struggle to control where their attention goes. Studies have shown that brains affected by ADHD have an unstable regulation of brain arousal (ADDitude Editors, 2024). This means that students with ADHD can become overstimulated much quicker than other students and they find it difficult to block out or control distractions.

Imagine for a second that you were attempting to listen to a student's question but your mind is also eavesdropping on a side conversation that other students are having and equally curious about the sound of birds chirping outside the classroom. Students with ADHD have split focus and get easily pulled by different stimuli in their environment. To get them to listen exclusively to you and drown the noise of everything else is not as simple as saying, "Focus, please!" Their brains need to be incentivized to focus their attention on one thing only.

Here are strategies on how you can help students improve their focus:

Self-Monitoring

Teach students how to notice when they have become distracted and gently redirect their attention to the task in front of them. For example, as soon as their eyes move away from the classwork, that means they have found a distraction. When they become aware of this, ask them to close their eyes and take a deep breath, then fix their eyes back on the classwork and start working again. If they are distracted while listening to you give instructions, ask them to focus on a specific part of your face, like your eyes or forehead. Taking deep breaths before refocusing allows them to regain control of their attention.

Choose Seating Wisely

Students with attention challenges should ideally sit in the front of the class where distractions are limited. They may also be encouraged to focus when seated within close distance to your (or their teacher's) desks and away from windows and doors.

Whenever you notice that their mind has drifted, you can calmly call their name and redirect their attention to the assignment.

Redirect Rather Than Reprimand

It can be frustrating to stand in front of the class and see students' eyes wandering to different parts of the classroom and not focus on you. However, many times, the mind wandering is not something that students with ADHD can control. Reprimanding them every time they get distracted can be embarrassing and shattering to their self-confidence. Instead, you can interrupt their mind wandering by redirecting their attention to the appropriate task. Calling their name and asking a question or lightly patting them on the shoulder can wake them up and help them refocus on the task.

Make Learning Interesting

Find creative and diverse ways of presenting information to keep learning fun, interactive, and engaging. Your challenge is to appeal to your students' senses and accommodate different learning styles. For instance, your lessons can incorporate various forms of multimedia, such as written text, imagery, video, and audio. Bringing these multimedia elements together creates an entertaining and stimulating learning experience.

Group Activity: Create a Structured Environment

With the help of other teachers, go inside a teacher's classroom and identify quick improvements that you can make to create a more structured environment. For instance, you can rearrange seats, organize toys and books in one area, include more charts and visual aids, and so on.

Individual Activity: Attention-Focusing Meditation

Complete the following guided meditation to experience firsthand the benefits of redirection.

Record yourself repeating the following instructions with an audio recording device, then sit down in a quiet room and follow the guided meditation:

- Set a stopwatch for five minutes.

- Find a comfortable sitting position and close your eyes.

- Feel the weight of your body pressing against the chair or floor. Relax your muscles and allow your arms and shoulders to drop naturally.

- Focus your attention on your breathing. Take deep breaths through your nose and out of your mouth. Inhale for five counts, hold your breath for five counts, then exhale for five counts. Repeat this breathing sequence over and over again.

- It is normal for your mind to get distracted by thoughts, sensations, sounds, or movements happening around you. When your mind wanders, gently redirect your attention to your breathing.

- When the five minutes is over, take a deep breath, and open your eyes.

What's important to remember about students with attention difficulties is that they do desire to focus in class, however, their minds are constantly presenting stimuli. Being considerate of their challenges and working around them can help them reduce the stress that comes with ongoing distractions and promote engagement.

Now let's move on to the following chapter which will present classroom strategies to manage hyperactivity and impulsivity.

Chapter 6:

Managing Impulsivity and Hyperactivity

Be patient with me. Understand why I do the things I do. Don't yell at me. Believe me, I don't want to have ADHD. –Joane E. Richardson

Hyperactivity and Impulsivity in the Classroom

ADHD is commonly recognized as hyperactivity and impulsivity. You may find it easier to identify students who have this presentation of ADHD over students who have inattentive ADHD. Nevertheless, accommodations need to be made for both types of students to provide equal access and opportunities for learning.

Hyperactivity and impulsivity are as chaotic as you might think. Depending on the student's age, they may exhibit all kinds of active and disruptive behaviors, such as wanting to be the center of attention, interrupting others while they speak, refusing to share or wait for their turn, and performing inappropriate movements in the classroom like running or standing on their seat.

The classroom environment is not designed to accommodate these energetic and unrestrained behaviors. In a structured classroom, there will be clear rules and instructions that require focus and subdued energy. Students who go against these standards are seen as being troublesome.

Instructing students who are hyperactive and impulsive isn't easy. Even though you desire to be inclusive and enforce classroom expectations for all students to follow, students who have hyperactive ADHD struggle to meet those expectations and subsequently isolate themselves from the rest of the group. Their disruptive behaviors may cause disharmony in the classroom and place a strain on their relationships, which often leads to them being disciplined frequently, getting low grades, being bullied by their peers, and having low self-esteem.

In this chapter, we are going to look at effective strategies to help your students manage their hyperactive and impulsive behaviors so they can feel included and confident in the classroom. The strategies apply to students in general and are not specific to any grade.

Teaching Self-Regulation Strategies

Self-regulation refers to being in control of your thoughts, emotions, and behaviors. This skill is crucial for students with ADHD, whose brains have trouble paying attention and managing urges and impulses. Unlike other students, they have a hard time getting their minds and bodies to follow instructions. Self-regulation is also a necessary component for memory recall and learning, which means that students with poor self-regulation will likely have challenges concentrating during lessons, completing homework, studying for tests, and memorizing information.

No child is born with self-regulation skills. From the moment an infant comes out of their mother's womb, they are kicking and screaming. Self-regulation must be taught and reinforced both at school and at home to neurotypical and neurodivergent children. Research shows that the earlier a child learns how to self-regulate, the better their health and academic performance will be later in life (Copper, 2018). Regardless of what age or grade your students are in, you can start teaching self-regulation skills by incorporating them into your lessons. When doing so, it is important to emphasize the following cognitive processes that reinforce self-regulation:

- **Inhibition:** The ability to monitor and control your thoughts and emotions, and display appropriate social behaviors.

- **Problem-solving and organizational skills:** Learning how to define problems, brainstorm solutions, and create structured plans and routines to address common challenges.

- **Emotional regulation:** The ability to identify, label, and describe emotions, and handle them in healthy ways.

- **Working memory:** The practice of recalling information that you have recently learned and being able to apply the information to current situations.

There are fun ways to teach self-regulation without making it obvious to your students that you are strengthening their cognitive function. Below are some strategies that you can modify and implement in your classroom.

Model Self-Regulation

Model what self-regulation looks like by adopting healthy habits that enable you to manage stress and triggers. For example, when a student has made you upset, excuse yourself from the class and spend a few minutes taking deep breaths. Return to the classroom when you are feeling grounded. Explain to your students that you were feeling upset and needed to take a few moments to cool down. With a level head, address the inappropriate behavior and enforce the necessary consequences.

Create Predictable Classroom Routines

Students with ADHD have a difficult time managing transitions. Having predictable routines can help them anticipate what is coming and mentally prepare themselves. You can establish predictability by following a similar structure for your lessons. For example, the first part of your lesson could involve giving instructions, the second part could involve engaging with the content, and the third part could involve a short assessment to reinforce the key concepts. There will be no surprises when students are asked to complete the assessments at the end because they are accustomed to the routine. Plus, knowing that there is an assessment coming up could enhance their level of focus during the lesson.

Teach Emotional Recognition and Expression

Big emotions like anger, sadness, boredom, or loneliness can be overwhelming for students who haven't learned how to recognize and express their feelings. When they learn about these different emotions and have the correct vocabulary to name and describe them, they can feel a greater sense of control when they emerge. Encourage your students to name and describe how they are feeling every day. This can be done by creating rituals. For instance, in the mornings when students enter the classroom you can ask how they are feeling. After completing tests or learning new concepts, you have another opportunity to ask students how they feel. Hang up emotion charts around the classroom that visually depict different emotions and help students assess the intensity of their emotions.

Use Positive Reinforcement

Controlling strong urges and emotions is tough and acknowledging your student's efforts whenever they perform expected behaviors can motivate them to keep trying. Positive reinforcement involves praising and showing appreciation for the behaviors you would like to see happening more often. For this strategy to be effective, you must catch your students in the act of doing something that you approve of and offer praise. For example, when you see a student raising their hand instead of blurting out the answer, take a moment immediately afterward to recognize their good behavior and thank them. When a student who normally submits incomplete assignments unexpectedly submits a completed assignment, call them aside and acknowledge their outstanding behavior.

Create a Calm-Down Area

It is common for students with hyperactivity to feel restless and overwhelmed. Sometimes, their disruptive behaviors are a result of boredom or being overstimulated. A calm-down area is a section in the classroom designed to help overstimulated students calm down. You can decide what to include in the section, such as comfortable bean bags, stuffed animals, and books. The moment you notice changes in a student's moods (i.e. going from being cooperative to increasingly loud and uncooperative), go down to their level and ask how they are feeling. Validate their emotions and suggest sitting in the calm-down area for five minutes.

Encourage Positive Self-Talk

Hyperactive students can behave appropriately in the classroom, however, they must believe that they can. Behaviors do not function independently from thoughts and beliefs. When students believe they can change, changes start to happen. Positive self-talk is a technique that promotes compassionate internal dialogue. Over time, this can lead to increased self-control and emotional resilience. Create a large colorful chart with 10 positive statements that students can repeat to themselves daily. The statements should reinforce their strengths, capabilities, and positive mindset. Here are examples of 10 statements that promote positive self-talk:

1. Every day presents an opportunity to start over.

2. I am doing the best I can.

3. I make myself proud.

4. It's okay to feel the way I feel.

5. I am stronger than I was yesterday.

6. I can do anything I put my mind to.

7. I love learning new things.

8. I choose to be happy.

9. My thoughts are important.

10. I am in charge of my choices.

Implementing Environmental Modifications

Due to the poor regulation of brain arousal, students with ADHD tend to experience sensory overload. The sounds, voices, lights, textures, and smells coming from all corners of the classroom cause them to lose focus and become agitated. Neurotypical students have the cognitive capacity to process large volumes of sensory information from their surroundings, but neurodivergent students cannot process it all at once. Making a few environmental modifications can reduce the *sensory noise* that so often distracts and frustrates students with ADHD.

Here are some recommendations on how you can modify the classroom to create a pleasant sensory experience for your students:

Temperature Considerations

A classroom that is too hot or too cold can trigger sensory overwhelm and lead to heightened sensitivity, lethargy, and irritability. Your students could be so distracted by the temperature that they lose focus on the lesson. Find the perfect balance between hot and cold temperatures that is cool and comfortable for your students. In colder seasons, encourage your students to bring a blanket to class or wear an extra layer of clothing. In warmer seasons, open the windows, put on the fan, and encourage your students to carry a bottle of water.

Lighting Considerations

Good lighting is essential in the classroom, however, lights that are too dim or too bright can be distracting for students with ADHD. In general, lighting should not put a strain on your students' eyes. The best type of lighting solution mimics natural daylight. It is not blinding, blurry, or dim. Natural daylight is known to enhance moods and induce a sense of alertness and focus. Replace your classroom bulbs with adjustable LED lights that can be turned up or down to create the perfect daylight effect.

Noise Considerations

Noises inside a classroom do not only come from the educator and students talking. Noise can also come from technological devices, furniture, stationery supplies, and movements like dropping books, crinkling paper, whispering, and coughing. All of these noises are sensed by students with ADHD, and over time, they can become sources of distraction. Do your best to reduce as much noise as you can inside your classroom by switching to carpet floors, plugging in a white noise machine, or asking students to leave their school bags outside of the classroom and only bring the textbooks and stationery supplies they will need. You can also monitor and limit student conversations during work times.

Classroom Layout Considerations

Students with hyperactive ADHD need to stand up and move around. Modifying your classroom layout can ensure that they don't hurt themselves or feel restricted when moving up and down. An ADHD-friendly layout provides clear pathways to the teacher's desk, front of the classroom, and entrance/exit doors. It also creates designated areas for working, taking breaks, and having one-on-one sessions with the teacher. Seating arrangements are designed to limit distractions and socializing during class time.

Providing Visual Aids

Having a variety of visual aids in the classroom can improve learning and engagement. Oftentimes, students with ADHD lose focus when a teacher is lecturing in front of the class, especially when it has continued for several minutes without any active engagement. Supplementing learning with visual aids ensures that even when students are distracted, they have charts, infographics, and color-coded systems to help them retain information. You can also encourage students to create their own visual aids when learning for tests and exams. This could be as simple as drawing a picture or table that helps them organize information better.

Group Activity: Student-Teacher Role-Play

Sit in pairs as teachers and role-play scenarios involving a hyperactive student and a teacher. Practice different ways to respond calmly to the student and teach them self-regulation strategies. Switch roles so that each person gets to play the role of the teacher.

Individual Activity: Classroom Environment Walkthrough

Conduct a walkthrough inside your classroom and look for potential environmental triggers that can lead to sensory overload. Brainstorm appropriate modifications that you can make to minimize distractions and create a harmonious environment.

As a teacher, you expect students to come to class ready to learn. However, some students, particularly those who live with ADHD, may not always come prepared. Teaching and reinforcing self-regulation skills can help students with hyperactive ADHD manage their urges, emotions, and behaviors. This ensures that they have fewer distractions to worry about that could get in the way of absorbing information. The next chapter discusses strategies to teach executive function skills in the classroom.

Chapter 7:

Addressing Executive Functioning Challenges

It is difficult to instruct children because of their natural inattention; the true mode, of course, is to first make our modes interesting to them. —
John Locke

What Are Executive Functioning Skills?

ADHD is a neurological disorder that causes changes in the size and function of the brain. One of the brain areas that are severely impacted is the prefrontal cortex. The prefrontal cortex sits at the front of the brain and regulates your thoughts, emotions, and behaviors. Impairments to the prefrontal cortex can cause dysregulation in the way you think, feel, and behave.

The prefrontal cortex is also responsible for regulating executive functioning skills, which are a set of skills that help you think critically, process and memorize information, solve problems, follow instructions, and execute goals. Students with ADHD, both those with inattentive and hyperactive ADHD, suffer from poor executive functioning skills due to impairments to their prefrontal cortex. Subsequently, they experience challenges when it comes to staying organized, concentrating on tasks, controlling emotions and impulses, following rules, and so on.

What's important to emphasize is that nobody is born with executive functioning skills. Similar to self-regulation skills (a type of executive functioning skill), they must be taught and reinforced at school and home. However, students with ADHD experience delays in learning these executive functioning skills. This means that their skills may not be appropriate for their age. Eventually, they will catch up, but not without additional support from teachers.

Common Executive Functioning Deficits of Students With ADHD

Having a clear understanding of the specific executive functioning deficits that your students have can make providing targeted support much easier. There are specific deficits that are common among students with ADHD, regardless of their age or gender. These include:

Difficulty With Self-Guided Learning

We all have an inner voice or coach inside our heads that guides us on what decisions to make or behaviors to avoid. In children with ADHD, this inner voice or coach is muted or turned down very low. What this means is that students have trouble identifying, monitoring, and correcting their behaviors. For instance, they might get reprimanded for talking loudly in class today but carry out the same behavior tomorrow.

Difficulty With Future Thinking Skills

Children with ADHD have a hard time connecting the actions of today with the outcomes of tomorrow. For instance, students may not be able to understand how studying two weeks before the test will help them achieve a better grade. The time horizon is too far for them to feel motivated to modify their behaviors and visualize the long-term rewards.

Difficulty With Time Management

It is common for students with ADHD to struggle with time management because they don't have a sense of the passage of time. As a result, deadlines don't create a sense of urgency or lead to better organizational skills. They may only feel the urge to take action when the deadline is fast approaching.

Difficulty Sustaining Focus With Non-Preferred Tasks

Students with ADHD are driven by emotion more than logic. They tend to make decisions based on how good or bad they feel. For instance, you may notice that students perform better on subjects they prefer or activities they find interesting. However, when it comes to their least favorite subjects or tasks they find boring or complicated, they don't put as much effort into their work. Making the transition from a preferred task to a non-preferred task can also be difficult for students (especially when they are not prepared for it). They might complain, make excuses, or seem disengaged.

When students are not taught how to manage these deficits and develop their executive functioning skills, they can become overly dependent on you as their teacher to complete their executive functioning on their behalf. For example, younger students may expect you to help them regulate their strong emotions and older students may expect you to constantly remind them of deadlines so they can stay organized. To empower your students to develop these skills on their own, you can train them through a technique called scaffolding.

Scaffolding refers to establishing a structure or framework that can help students learn and practice executive functioning skills over time, at their own pace. Your job is to offer support by encouraging skills-based games, breaking down processes into smaller steps or tasks, setting rules and enforcing consequences, and promoting creative problem-solving. In other words, you provide the necessary tools for them to learn executive functioning skills, and then step back and play a supportive role.

How to Teach Executive Functioning Skills?

It is worth emphasizing that executive functioning skills are essential for learning. without these skills, students may struggle to succeed in higher grades. The lack of critical thinking and emotional skills can lead to academic delays and difficulties, as well as social and interpersonal challenges.

Fortunately, the classroom environment promotes the learning and practice of executive functioning skills through classwork, meaningful exchanges between students and teachers, and peer relationships. Examples of skills that are taught in the classroom include:

- **Planning:** Students are urged to write down deadlines, create homework timetables, and schedule time to work on projects or study for upcoming tests.

- **Organization:** Students are required to keep their workspace neat and use files and other storage folders to keep their schoolwork and test records.

- **Time management:** Students are encouraged to arrive on time to class, complete classwork before the bell rings, and allocate some time in the afternoons to complete homework.

- **Self-monitoring:** Students are required to uphold classroom rules and etiquette, come up with solutions to problems they have caused (e.g. forgetting textbook at home), and adjust their behaviors to nurture peer relationships (e.g. practicing taking turns listening and speaking).

The opportunity you have as a teacher is to find different ways of reinforcing these skills in the classroom so that they become automatic behaviors for students. With that said, please note that students develop executive functioning skills at different speeds and some may require additional support to build them. Furthermore, stress and anxiety interfere with the learning process and can delay the adoption of executive functioning skills.

If you are aware that one or some of your students with ADHD are struggling with executive functioning skills to the extent of negatively impacting their learning, consider speaking with their parents and discussing options for individualized support and special education services. Be on the lookout for students who are severely stressed due to school demands or personal conflict at home, as these stressors can interfere with their executive functioning.

Effective Executive Functioning Strategies to Incorporate in the Classroom

Below are useful scaffolding strategies that can help your students learn and practice executive functioning skills:

Role-Play Using Real-Life Scenarios

Earlier we mentioned that students with ADHD struggle to plan for the future and modify their behaviors accordingly. Role-playing can help them learn this skill and imagine how they would tackle a real-life scenario.

For example, when there is a big test coming up, you can ask students to imagine the best time in the afternoons to study for the test. Discuss possible challenges that might prevent them from committing to studying, such as attending a sports match, taking a nap, or feeling demotivated.

Brainstorm alternative solutions that could work, such as studying before taking a nap. Go over the consequences of not putting in enough time to study for the test. Explore the possible negative outcomes with them and weigh the impact.

Self-Directed Goal Setting

Help your students become more organized by teaching them how to set meaningful goals and execute them. Use the SMART goal-setting framework to walk students through the process of creating achievable goals. The framework includes five steps that students can complete on their own:

- **Specific:** Define what you want to achieve using clear and simple language. Focus on a specific objective that can improve your learning experience.

- **Measurable:** Consider how you are going to measure your progress. For instance, is there a specific target you want to reach? Clearly state what that target is.

- **Achievable:** Determine whether the goal you have set is within your reach. In other words, do you have the necessary tools and materials to work on your goal?

- **Relevant:** The goal needs to be something that personally impacts your life. Look over the goal again and determine if it is something that adds value to your education.

- **Time-bound:** Set a realistic deadline to achieve your goal. When setting a deadline, consider the weeks or months you will need to spend practicing certain skills and tasks.

Breaking down Goals Into Smaller Tasks

Once your students have learned how to set SMART goals, teach them how to map out the process to achieve their goals. A simple technique is to brainstorm the smaller tasks that will need to be practiced once or continually to achieve goals. Get your students to write down as many tasks as they can think of related to the goal.

Thereafter, ask them to draw a table with four columns and group the tasks under four categories: once-off, daily, weekly, and monthly tasks. Instead of focusing on executing the big goal, encourage them to focus on completing once-off, daily, weekly, and monthly tasks. At the end of the day, week, or month, they can assess how many tasks they were able to complete successfully. This extra step promotes accountability.

Allow Time for Organization During Class

Your students may struggle to keep their workspaces neat, especially on days when they are engaging in creative tasks or group projects. To reinforce the importance of a clean and orderly space, allocate a few minutes during class for organization. You can call this *clean-up time* or *decluttering time*. For 2-5 minutes, allow students to move around and clean up their workspaces, put books away, throw papers in the trash, and wipe their desks. For older students, this time could also be used to write down their homework in their school diaries, create to-do lists, review upcoming deadlines, submit assignments, and ask any questions relating to schoolwork and expectations.

Use Timers

Timers can help students stay focused on tasks and plan their time effectively. Whenever students are about to start a task, communicate how much time you are giving them to complete it. Start the timer and notify them when they have five minutes remaining. At first, your students may not understand the significance of five minutes, but with time, they will be able to work diligently. Timers can also be used to create fun challenges. For example, you might give your students three open-book questions and challenge them to complete the answers within three minutes. With older students, you can ask them how much time they will need to complete a class assignment and then set a timer. This can empower them to take ownership of their time.

State When You Are Sharing Important Information

One of the ways to increase alertness and promote working memory is to be deliberate when sharing information that students need to remember for future classwork and assessments. For instance, while giving instructions, you might pause and say "This next section that we are about to cover is extremely important for your upcoming test. Please pay attention and take notes." If you wish, you can also provide students with examples of how information might be presented in an exam situation. Before assessments, provide students with a scope of topics to study. Once again, this can help them direct their focus on specific content and manage their time effectively.

Explain Rubrics and Criteria for Success

Whenever students are required to submit assignments that will be graded, spend some time going over the rubrics with them so they get a clear understanding of the quality of work and level of detail expected. Read the criteria for achieving the highest and lowest scores and offer examples of the outstanding or poor quality of work that might cause students to get those grades. Allow students to ask questions and clarify any misunderstanding related to rubrics.

Group Activity: Executive Function Lesson Plan

Sit with a group of teachers who teach students of similar ages and grades and compile a lesson plan based on teaching various executive functioning skills. Use the information included in this chapter to design the lesson plan. Interested teachers can use the lesson plan as part of their teaching.

Individual Activity: Exploring Executive Functioning Tools

Conduct research and identify executive functioning tools and strategies that you can introduce to your students. Go online and look up popular games or technological apps that are helpful for students. Reflect on how you can integrate these tools and strategies into your classroom instruction and lessons.

Nobody is born with executive functioning skills, however, they are essential to succeeding at school and other aspects of life. Students with ADHD have delayed executive functioning skills and may have difficulty planning, staying organized, regulating emotions, and memorizing information. By teaching and reinforcing executive functioning skills using the scaffolding technique, you can empower students to develop these skills over time.

Let's move on to the next chapter which explores social skills and strategies you can teach students to improve their peer relationships.

Chapter 8:

Social Skills Development and Peer Interactions

High stimulation is both exciting and confusing for people with ADHD, because they can get overwhelmed and overstimulated easily without realizing they are approaching that point. –Jenara Nerenberg

ADHD and Peer Relationships

Human beings are social creatures who thrive in groups rather than in isolation. Forming healthy relationships with others fulfills our need for a sense of belonging and acceptance. Adults have experience in social relations and could be more selective about who they hang around and when they choose to socialize. However, children depend on social interactions to feel competent and confident in themselves.

Social skills refer to the set of skills that build and improve interpersonal relationships. They include both verbal and nonverbal communication, as well as social awareness of the dynamics of our environment. Children develop social skills on the playground or playpen when they interact with other children. With the guidance of an adult, they can learn how to share toys, take turns, initiate conversations, and resolve conflict.

Students with ADHD struggle with social skills due to impairments in their prefrontal cortex and executive functioning. They are not aware of how to navigate relationships and may not always pick up on social cues. This makes them come across as socially awkward to others, which impacts the degree of acceptance they receive from peers. Furthermore, ADHD symptoms can create unique social challenges that further complicate peer relationships. Here are some of the social difficulties that are presented with inattentiveness, hyperactivity, and impulsivity:

Inattentiveness

- difficulty paying attention to what others are saying

- hearing some pieces of information but missing others

- getting distracted while others are speaking

- difficulty reading facial expressions and body language

- being overwhelmed in social settings and withdrawing from others

- missing important social cues (e.g. recognizing when someone is uncomfortable)

Hyperactivity

- frequently interrupting others while they are speaking
- speaking without organizing thoughts and presenting clear ideas
- seeking to be the center of attention in conversations
- talking fast and incoherently
- speaking excessively without giving others a turn
- difficulty regulating the tone and volume of speech

Impulsivity

- laughing or making jokes at inappropriate times
- blurting out rude words or insults
- interrupting other people's conversations
- frequently arguing or debating with others
- humming and making strange noises randomly
- initiating conversations at inappropriate times (e.g. speaking in the library)

Students with ADHD desire meaningful relationships just like any other young person. They often watch as their peers bounce energy off each other, share inside jokes, and build camaraderie, and they secretly yearn for the same type of bond. The challenge that students with ADHD have is learning the appropriate social behavior and how to communicate effectively.

As an educator, you play a crucial role in helping all students feel included and accepted in your classroom. Students with ADHD require more assistance to build and nurture peer relationships. They need to be taught executive functioning skills like self-monitoring and emotional regulation that can help them avoid making *social faux pas* such as looking disinterested, getting distracted, being impatient, or saying the wrong things.

How to Teach Social Skills?

Sociable students build strong peer relationships and learn vital skills like how to negotiate, cooperate, solve problems, and work as a team. These skills are not only useful in social settings but they also enhance learning in the classroom. There is a correlation between social skills and academic performance. For instance, the ability to cooperate with others can help students follow instructions and submit classwork on time. The ability to empathize with others can improve collaboration on group projects, increase participation in class discussions, and reduce unwanted behaviors.

There are a few considerations that you need to make before going full force into teaching students with ADHD effective social skills. The first is that social skills won't cure ADHD symptoms. Students may show improvements in the way they interact with others, however, they may continue to struggle with attention, distractions, and impulsivity. Don't be discouraged when you notice inappropriate social behavior after all the work you have put in. Your students may be going through a stressful period, which aggravates their ADHD symptoms and makes them harder to manage.

Second, social skills won't change your students' personalities. Their sharp tongue or fear of talking could be personality traits that they were born with. The best you can do is teach them how to be socially aware of their pleasant and unpleasant traits and how others perceive them. For example, a student with a sharp tongue may cause their peers to feel offended, and as a result, they might lose friends. With greater social awareness, the student can learn to be more careful with how they speak to others.

Lastly, it is important to use the scaffolding technique when teaching social skills so that your students do not become dependent on your assistance to build and nurture relationships. You cannot make friends on their behalf or resolve every conflict they start. The responsibility to develop and practice social skills lies with them.

Strategies to Facilitate Peer Relationships

The advantage you have as a teacher is that your students feel safe and comfortable talking to you. This means that you can build strong relationships and learn enough about them to identify their social challenges. Using scaffolding and fun social activities, you can help students enhance their social skills and strengthen peer relationships.

Here are some strategies that you can practice with your students:

Model Good Manners

Effective communication starts with having good manners, like saying please and thank you. Show your students what good manners look like by modeling them in the classroom. Every morning, greet your students with a warm smile and a kind tone of voice and prompt them to respond the same to you. When making requests, say please and thank you. Even when you are frustrated, maintain a calm and respectful tone of voice to show your students a positive way of addressing conflict. Hang up a poster with a list of good manners so that your students are aware of the communication behaviors expected of them.

Assign Classroom Duties to Students

Self-confidence is connected to competence. When students complete tasks, they feel a sense of accomplishment which boosts confidence. Have your students help out in the classroom by assigning them classroom duties to complete in pairs. Each week assign a different pair of students to manage a simple classroom task, such as handing out papers, monitoring the noise levels, taking class attendance, or reading announcements. Make sure that every student gets an opportunity to participate. Create a roster so that you can prepare students a week in advance when it is going to be their turn.

Pen Pals

Set up a pen pal program with students from a different school. Decide on the medium of writing (e.g. electronic or paper) and how frequently letters will be exchanged. The pen pal program enhances students' vocabulary, language abilities, and creative writing skills. They also get a chance to reflect on their thoughts and emotions and empathize with the realities of other people. This activity levels the playing field for introverted and extroverted students and creates a positive experience that students can talk about with each other. Before you introduce the program to your students, make sure that you have considered their safety and privacy and have a comprehensive set of guidelines for sharing content.

Buddy System

Sometimes, students with ADHD may feel pressure to socialize with peers who are on the same level, since their executive functioning skills are delayed. Instead, they may feel comfortable building relationships with students in lower grades who they may have more in common with. The buddy system is a mentoring program that pairs students in higher grades with students in lower grades within the same school. Teachers from both classrooms meet and decide on the pairing, and then facilitate the friendly meetings. During buddy meetings, older students can bring a book to read to the younger students or have several games to play.

Class Meetings

Classroom meetings bring students together and teach them how to take turns speaking and be diplomatic in the way they solve problems. Meetings can take place weekly or monthly, at the start or end of the lesson. In elementary and middle school, teachers must lead the discussions and offer opportunities for students to raise their hands and share their thoughts. However, in high school, teachers can give students turns to lead the discussions. To help students lead the meetings effectively, read out the rules for the meeting and provide a copy of sentence prompts to drive questions. Various topics can be discussed at these meetings including upcoming tests and deadlines, current student issues, or suggestions for fun events and projects.

Provide Opportunities to Connect

It is rare for students to go out of their way to get to know classmates. They are more likely to interact with peers when they have already formed a relationship outside of the classroom or have worked with them before on group projects. Create opportunities for students to interact by incorporating group activities in your lessons and promoting a culture of teamwork and collaboration in the classroom. For example, encourage your students to lean on each other when they need support by asking for help. You can also motivate students to celebrate each other's achievements by driving a student of the week or month initiative. The prize winner should be a student who has demonstrated kindness and good teamwork over the period.

Role Play Scenarios

If you notice a student who is seriously struggling to make friends, you can work with them on a one-on-one basis and role-play different social scenarios. Go back and forth with each other in different ways to respond in social settings. Present real-life scenarios that they come across every day and practice positive social skills. For example, you might role-play greeting peers in the mornings, asking to join a group, offering compliments, and asking open-ended questions to drive conversations. Print out conversational scripts that the students can practice with you in the classroom and when they get home. Meet regularly and review progress.

Group Activity: Classroom Culture

Discuss and brainstorm a positive culture to establish in the classroom that promotes a sense of community and belonging.

Reflect on the core values that are essential for achieving this vision. Work together to create a code of conduct that promotes this culture. Think of social strategies that can help you reinforce the culture in your respective classrooms.

Individual Activity: Social Skills Observation

For a week, observe students' peer interactions inside the classroom or during recess. Make notes of the negative social behaviors that you find. Identify areas of improvement and social skills that are lacking, then create lessons centered around reinforcing those skills.

Social skills are important for strengthening peer relationships and enhancing academic performance. Students with ADHD require additional support in developing these skills and nurturing their relationships. Use the scaffolding technique to introduce and reinforce social skills during classroom encounters.

We have now completed the second part of the book which offered several classroom strategies for managing ADHD behaviors. Let us proceed to the third part of the book which explores ADHD-friendly communication techniques to use in the classroom.

PART 3:

ADHD-Friendly Communication in the Classroom

Chapter 9:

Clear and Concise Instruction

People with ADHD often have a special feel for life, a way of seeing right into the heart of matters, while others have to reason their way methodically. –Edward M. Hallowell

ADHD and Focus

Michael is a 10-year-old boy with hyperactive ADHD, who has difficulty following directions. Shortly after receiving detailed instructions, he stares at the assignment, unable to take action. Looking around in the class, he can see that all of the other students are engaged with the task at hand, but due to his disorder, he struggles to make the shift from intent to action.

His inability to pay attention to single tasks for long periods is also to blame. Once he finally starts an assignment, he will get distracted by the coughing or whispers coming from different parts of the classroom. Before long, he finds another distraction—perhaps a strange bump at the back of his neck which he hadn't noticed before. His focus is turned toward investigating what might have caused this bump and if it is something to worry about.

Michael's mental drifting is always interrupted by his teacher, standing over him with both hands on her hips. That's when it registers to him that he has made a mistake. Without saying any words, he looks back down at his barely started assignment and hopes this will be the last time his mind wanders.

Students with ADHD are known to forget instructions or have a hard time following them. You may have noticed that you have to follow after your students, asking how far they are with their tasks, reminding them of the steps to take, and redirecting their attention to their classwork. The constant follow-ups can get frustrating, especially when students don't seem engaged with their work.

The lack of focus is a common ADHD symptom that affects children of all ages. It is caused by inattentiveness, distractibility, and hyperactivity. Students may only be able to concentrate for a few minutes at a time before shifting their focus to something else. However, interestingly, when engaging in subjects or activities they find stimulating, students may display hyperfocus and block out everything else.

Getting students with ADHD to focus on tasks they dislike is exceptionally challenging. One scientific explanation for this is that ADHD interferes with the production of hormones, including dopamine (Green, 2024). Dopamine is known as the *feel-good* brain chemical that enhances moods and drives motivation. Low levels of dopamine affect the desire and drive to perform tasks. Since students with ADHD already have low levels of dopamine, pushing themselves to complete undesirable tasks requires a great deal of effort. Examples of undesirable tasks include reading, long homework assignments, learning a new skill, preparing for a test in the future, and repetitive tasks.

The inability to focus impacts students' academic performance. For instance, they may start a task but struggle to complete it on time, or they may start a task and get distracted by something they find more entertaining. Sometimes students may become hyperfocused on a particular topic or skill they enjoy and not invest as much time and energy on topics and skills they find boring or difficult. Over time, the lack of focus leads to forgetfulness or skipping important steps, making careless mistakes, difficulty listening attentively, and re-reading instructions because of not being able to absorb information.

You may not be able to completely fix students' lack of focus, but you can modify the way you provide instructions to assist students with attention challenges. In this chapter, we will look at two effective strategies that can help you achieve that.

How to Simplify Instructions?

Trouble with focus makes following instructions tough. This becomes even harder when instructions are vague, too long, or too complicated. Simplifying instructions will benefit not only students with ADHD but all students who require extra support to complete tasks. Here are some strategies that you can use to simplify instructions:

Be Precise

Make your instructions easy to follow by using precise language. It should be clear what the expectations are and how students can achieve them. If you are explaining how to complete a process, go through each step and provide examples. Avoid using questions when making requests, as this can sometimes cause students to think they have a choice. Instead of saying, "Can you please submit the assignment before the end of the day?" you can say "You are required to submit the assignment before the end of the day."

Give One or Two Directions at a Time

To avoid confusion and low morale, provide students with one or two steps to follow. Clearly state that they have one or two things to get done before the end of the day or week and explain precisely what they are. When students have a big project or assignment coming up, encourage them to break down the project or goal into smaller tasks and focus on one or two tasks per week. The same applies to studying; encourage students to focus on one or two topics each day when studying for an upcoming test.

Reinforce Verbal Instructions

Students will likely break focus at least once while you are giving verbal instructions. To make sure that they have heard and understood everything, find an additional way of reinforcing the instructions. For example, you may repeat the instructions by writing down the steps on a whiteboard, handing out papers that summarize what you spoke about, playing an educational animation video, or choosing random students to repeat the instructions to the rest of the class.

Strategies to Avoid Ambiguity

Students with ADHD may not necessarily have a language disorder, however, their attention challenges make it hard for them to process and understand language. Part of simplifying instructions involves using vocabulary that is familiar and easy to understand. You may also need to articulate yourself to make sure students don't miss any words. Here are some strategies that can help you speak more clearly:

Speak Slowly and Patiently

Never be in a rush to get through an instruction or explain a concept. Students with ADHD process information at such a rapid speed that they often miss important details. By deliberately slowing your pace and speaking with greater intention and clarity, you force students to lean closer and hold onto every word. Look at a mirror and practice giving instructions at your normal speaking pace and two or three paces slower. Don't speak too slowly so that you sound tired. Your voice should be soothing but energetic enough to keep students engaged.

Use Exaggerated Gestures

Students with ADHD crave stimulation. Their eyes gravitate to whatever they consider fascinating. To keep your students glued onto you, use your whole body to convey messages. For instance, speak with your eyes, eyebrows, mouth, arms, and hands. Make big and exaggerated gestures to drive important messages. For example, walk across the room instead of standing in one place and when emphasizing certain points, open your eyes and lean forward. Some of your gestures may incite laughter, but this is a positive sign of engagement!

Stop Frequently to Assess Understanding

You shouldn't assume that just because all students are looking at you they understand what you are saying. Some students may be looking at you but they are thinking of something else. Take frequent pauses when you are giving instructions to check if everyone is still following. You can ask, "Are there any questions?" or make the students give a thumbs up or thumbs down to show their understanding. You can also assess understanding by selecting students randomly to repeat the information. Go back as many times to explain concepts until everyone is satisfied. Use new examples or scenarios to present the information differently.

Play the "Repeat Back to Me" Game

The *repeat back to me* game is a form of parrot learning where students repeat the words and sentences that come out of your mouth. This happens at least three to five times to promote memory recall. During the first few rounds, students may be distracted or partially engaged, but the longer the game continues, the more focused they become. There is a good chance that they will remember the words or sentences long after they have left the class. To make the game more fun, create a melody or body movement that students can associate with the information.

Be Optimistic

When you communicate in a friendly and positive way, students feel calm and relaxed listening to you. They may also feel confident approaching you with questions when they don't understand certain concepts. Check on your mood before standing up in class to give instructions or respond to student questions. It is better to have a delayed positive response than a quick annoyed response. Your positive energy is transferable to students and their willingness to learn can be increased by your enthusiasm about the subject.

Provide Visual Support

Verbal instructions are great, however, they may not always accommodate students who are visual learners or those who need additional academic support. ADHD affects students' ability to process and retain information, hence providing visual support offers another opportunity for them to memorize information.

The type of visual aids that you choose will depend on the academic level of your students. The goal is to enhance the learning process by illustrating information in a way that is easiest to remember and understand. The visual aids that you go for should break down complex information and draw patterns that help students connect the dots for themselves.

Here is a list of visual aids that you can consider incorporating into your lessons:

Schedules

Scheduling involves structuring information in a way that makes sense and enables planning. When students look at schedules, they can prioritize tasks, create short and long-term goals, and manage their time effectively. There are several types of schedules that you can create, such as daily routines, calendars, and to-do lists.

Checklists

Checklists are a great way of collecting feedback and assessing understanding. They can help students recall important information, keep track of complete and incomplete tasks, and assess whether they have met expectations. Checklists also serve as reminders to get certain things done. Students hold themselves accountable by checking items that have been completed. Completing checklists brings a sense of satisfaction and motivates good habits.

Graphs

Graphs offer a simplified way of understanding complex information. They are suitable for illustrating quantitative data, such as percentages and population sizes. From looking at graphs, students can identify trends, patterns, and unique relationships between different data sets. This allows them to summarize the information into simple sentences and make logical conclusions.

Charts

Charts are useful when seeking to simplify processes that would otherwise be difficult to explain. The information is presented in a way that highlights cause and effect. For example, arrows and lines are elements used on charts to show the relationship between different concepts, or how one step leads to another. Examples of charts include flow charts, mind maps, and infographics.

Drawings

Drawings are images or abstract illustrations that help students remember information. They are often presented on posters and come with minimal text. The aim is for students to recall information by viewing the drawing or image. Drawings are also interesting to look at and are more likely to draw students' attention than other visual aids like graphs or checklists.

To make visual aids effective, avoid including too much information where they become confusing. Focus on a specific skill, concept, or message you want to send across and use simple designs. For inspiration, you can search online for visual ideas or purchase visual aids on websites that sell teaching materials and resources.

Group Activity: Creating Visual Aids

Think about a common scenario involving a student who struggles to follow directions. Brainstorm and create a visual aid that can offer assistance to the student. Choose the most appropriate type of visual aid to emphasize the message.

Individual Activity: Simplifying Lesson Plans

Review an upcoming lesson that you will present to your class. Look for ways to simplify the content, explanations, and instructions given. Present the revised lesson and observe how your students respond (e.g. how many students seem confused, ask the same questions, etc.).

It can be frustrating when students aren't paying attention in class. To minimize these unpleasant experiences, consider modifying how you give directions. Focus on clarity, precision, and simplicity when giving verbal instructions. Supplement verbal instructions with visual aids to improve the learning process. The next chapter discusses positive ways to give constructive feedback to students with ADHD.

Chapter 10:

Effective Feedback and Reinforcement

They said I could pass as normal, that I was clever and no one would ever know. They lied. Not about passing. The lie was hidden beneath, in the desire for me to be the same as them. I am extraordinary. They should have helped me soar, be more of me, not less. –Anna Whateley

ADHD and Rejection Sensitivity

You may have noticed that students with ADHD have strong emotional reactions to minor corrections of their behavior. Even something such as using a strong tone of voice can make them teary or angry. To other people, this reaction may look like attention-seeking behavior or failure to take accountability for their actions. However, there is a medical reason why students with ADHD respond this way to constructive feedback.

The psychological condition that explains this phenomenon is rejection-sensitive dysphoria (RSD). It is common among people living with ADHD and is characterized by an extreme sensitivity to criticism (or what may be perceived as criticism). The condition has not been listed on the DSM-5, however, it is recognized by therapists and counselors and can be treated with medication and psychotherapy.

Since this condition is not widely known, RSD is often identified by its symptoms. Signs that your students with ADHD may have RSD include displaying social anxiety, fear of failure, perfectionist thinking, and avoidance behaviors. Their aversion to criticism and rejection causes them to avoid situations that might lead to them. As a result, they may struggle to engage with others beyond the surface level or step outside their comfort zones.

RSD episodes are triggered by situations where students are told no, reprimanded, or given constructive feedback. In response to these situations, students may react with explosive emotions or become withdrawn and feel immense sadness. The brain region known as the amygdala, which is responsible for regulating emotions activates, and the prefrontal cortex which is responsible for logical thinking temporarily shuts down. You may also notice that students become visibly stressed or anxious.

After episodes, students tend to feel remorseful or ashamed of how they handled the situations. This causes more guilt, anger, and sad feelings. They desperately want to make things right but don't know how. Students who have RSD will likely also have a harsh inner critical voice that puts them down and makes comparisons with others. They might be preoccupied with their self-image or being validated by their teachers and peers. Receiving negative feedback can trigger feelings of personal inadequacy and low self-worth.

Learning that you may have students who are living with RSD allows you to modify how you give constructive feedback. Constructive feedback is not the same as criticism because instead of tearing students down, you are seeking to build them up. Nevertheless, to students with RSD, constructive feedback can be taken as criticism due to their heightened sensitivity to rejection. In this chapter, we will look at some of the strategies for providing positive feedback to minimize misunderstandings.

Providing Constructive Feedback

Students need timely and consistent feedback to determine whether they are making good progress on their schoolwork. Feedback can also be a way to motivate students to work harder or maintain their level of performance. The purpose of feedback isn't always to mention things that students are doing wrong. Sometimes feedback acknowledges improvements that students are making.

Generally, all feedback ought to be constructive, whether you are sharing good news or bad news. Your aim for providing feedback should be to support your students' learning by helping them identify blind spots and highlighting their strengths. Students should feel encouraged to work on their skills and do better after receiving feedback.

The word *constructive* comes from the root word construct. To construct something means to build it up. Likewise, constructive feedback builds up your students and empowers them to unleash their potential. Understanding how to give constructive feedback is a skill. For instance, the following factors need to be considered when offering constructive feedback:

Teachable Moment

Constructive feedback teaches students something they don't know. For example, you might explain, clarify a concept, suggest a different method, or provide exercises that students can practice at home. Students walk away knowing what is expected of them and how to improve moving forward.

Timely Response

Constructive feedback is given promptly, usually immediately or within days of students taking action. How soon you provide feedback is also dependent on each situation. For example, when a student behaves poorly in class, you can call them aside and address their behaviors immediately or after class. However, when a student has submitted an assignment, you may need a few days or a week to grade the assignment and offer feedback. The reason why prompt feedback is such a huge factor is that it highlights the relationship between cause and effect. Students can see for themselves what led to them being disciplined or getting a low score on a test.

Performance Review

Constructive feedback reviews students' performance so that they know where they stand in terms of their academic capacity. Some of the questions you will need to answer when offering feedback include:

- What did the student do well?

- What can't the student do?

- How can the student improve?

Please note that even when students have failed tests or behaved poorly, there is still something positive that you can highlight to show them that not all hope is lost. Giving students a glimmer of hope is sometimes all they need to believe in themselves.

How to Use the Feedback Sandwich Method?

Sandwiches are constructed with bread on the outer layers so that the filling inside can stay together. The feedback sandwich method is a constructive feedback technique that softens bad news by starting and ending with positive reinforcement. This method is suitable when you need to correct inappropriate behavior or address academic concerns. The hope is that by starting and ending with positive reinforcement, the "meat" of your conversations won't be taken too harshly by the student.

There are some pros and cons to using the feedback sandwich method. The pros are that you can increase students' confidence in their work and performance by mentioning both strengths and weaknesses. Moreover, they are likely to receive the bad news with a positive attitude when you have started by making them feel good about themselves. The release of dopamine triggered by positive reinforcement reduces combativeness and promotes engagement.

With that said, there are some cons to using this method. The biggest critique is that starting and ending with positive reinforcement can make students feel confused about what exactly they need to solve or change. Some students may hold onto the positives and brush over the negatives thereby failing to take accountability for their actions. Another critique is that vague or generic positive reinforcement can make students doubt your sincerity and feel patronized by the feedback. This leads to growing mistrust and disengagement when feedback is given.

Offering targeted and meaningful positive reinforcement can make the feedback sandwich method a success. Spend time observing your students and taking notes of their behaviors so that you can identify progress when it's made. The positive reinforcement given to each student should reflect the growth and changes you have observed over time, therefore making the praise authentic and meaningful.

You have a general understanding of what every student is capable of achieving. When you notice increased focus, productivity, or quality of work, make a note of it. Here is an example of how to use the feedback sandwich method with targeted and meaningful positive reinforcement:

- **Positive reinforcement:** I am delighted to see that you are less talkative during instruction time.

- **Bad news:** I would like to separate you from [classmate's name] because I notice you get distracted easily when sitting next to them.

- **Positive reinforcement:** I believe that your level of focus can skyrocket by switching your seating. I am excited to see you continue to improve!

Implementing Behavior Modification Techniques

In general, you want to limit the amount of times that you have to discipline students to avoid shattering their confidence. However, the only way you can prevent discipline is if students are well-behaved. Behavior modification techniques are positive strategies for promoting desirable behaviors and discouraging undesirable behaviors. Essentially, you are teaching your students how to behave appropriately and rewarding them every time they do.

Consider the following behavior modification techniques that you can apply to your classroom:

Be Thorough When Explaining and Reinforcing Rules

Classroom rules are the boundaries you set to guide students' behaviors. Make sure that all students understand what the rules are and how to uphold them. Find ways to reinforce the rules, such as having quizzes or reading the rules once a week to make sure they stay top of mind. You can also create competitions around following the rules that come with tangible rewards.

Look for Progress, Not Perfection

Students will make mistakes and behave poorly every once in a while. As mentioned earlier in the book, sometimes bad behavior is a positive sign of growth and development. Do not seek perfection from your students, such as expecting them to never make mistakes. Not only is the expectation unrealistic, but it can also create anxiety and hyperfocus around behavior.

Focus on the ratio of times students behave appropriately than when they behave inappropriately. If they are making progress instead of regressing, then there is nothing to be concerned about.

Create a Rewards System

Students love to be rewarded because it makes them feel competent, and competence leads to greater self-confidence. Instead of shining a spotlight on negative behavior, redirect your attention to positive behaviors, and offer rewards for them. Rewards systems are point or token systems that incentivize good behaviors. Decide on what type of behaviors you would like students to aim for and write them down on a rewards chart. Create guidelines on how students can earn points or tokens. For example, they might earn a point if they perform certain behaviors once a day or at least three times a week. Observe students' behaviors and keep a tally of how often they meet the expectations. Publicly display students' progress on the reward chart to motivate other students to adopt the same habits.

Correct Undesirable Behavior in Private

Older students in high school may get embarrassed whenever their behaviors are corrected in front of their peers. This may prompt them to get defensive or argumentative with you. Speaking to them aside after class when everyone has left can deliver positive results. With just the two of you in the classroom, they can be open and receptive to what you have to say. Furthermore, privacy creates an opportunity to probe deeper and find out what might be triggering their behaviors. The student will walk away feeling respected and motivated to adjust their behaviors.

Be Predictable

Decide on how you are going to address troublesome behaviors and apply the same strategies consistently. Using different methods can make it harder for students to take the discipline seriously. Moreover, they struggle to anticipate the consequences, which makes it difficult for them to monitor and manage their behaviors. The difference between acceptable and unacceptable behaviors must be clear, and the consequences for unacceptable behaviors should be communicated and enforced the same way, all of the time.

Group Activity: Feedback Analysis Role-Play

Have two teachers stand in the front of the class and role-play a scenario involving a student with ADHD receiving constructive feedback from their teacher regarding behavior or academic issues. The other teachers should watch the scenario play out and offer suggestions on how to improve the delivery of the feedback. Next, a different pair of teachers can stand up and complete the same exercise using a different scenario. Continue to do this until all the teachers have practiced giving constructive feedback and being evaluated by their peers.

Individual Activity: Reflection and Goal-Setting

Reflect on your own feedback and positive reinforcement practices. Identify what you do well and areas where you can improve. Create a meaningful goal that you can work on for the next month to polish the way you give feedback. At the end of the month, review the progress you have made.

Students with ADHD are sensitive to criticism and may get emotional at the slightest sign of disapproval. It is important to be intentional and compassionate in how you give constructive feedback to avoid misunderstandings. Practicing the feedback sandwich method can decrease defensiveness while promoting openness and engagement. The following chapter will teach you ways of strengthening your student-teacher relationship and nurturing trust.

Chapter 11:

Building Positive Student-Teacher Relationships

*The children who need love the most will always ask for it in the most unloving ways. —*Russel Barkley

Why do Positive Student-Teacher Relationships Matter?

Earlier in the book, we discussed the importance of peer relationships for the well-being and success of students with ADHD at school. However, in this chapter, we will look into the value and significance of a healthy and positive student-teacher relationship.

It is assumed that students naturally get along with teachers, and vice versa. However, this isn't always the case. Certainly, teachers are professional and show respect for all students in their classroom, but these efforts don't always lead to close and trusting relationships. Like any other type of relationship, the student-teacher relationship takes a lot of work to build.

Consider the fact that outside of the classroom, you may not have personal contact with your students. This means that your relationships need to be built and nurtured during class time. It can be tricky to juggle doing your professional duties and forging meaningful relationships with every student in your class at the same time. To make it work, you may need to look for opportunities during your engagements to make students feel seen and accepted for who they are.

The impact of positive student-teacher relationships on students with ADHD can be astounding. Feeling a strong personal connection to you can encourage students to seek help when they need it and modify their behaviors to make you proud. Your students seek validation from you as much as you sometimes seek validation from them. Building open and honest relationships allows for both parties to fulfill their needs.

Mentally picture a student who looks forward to coming to class because they get to share a joke with you or tell you another story about their strange pets. Their friendly and open demeanor toward you allows them to share their thoughts and feelings freely. On days when they are acting out of character, you can call them aside and ask how they are doing instead of being quick to discipline them. When they are struggling with classwork, you can see it in their eyes and can offer support before they have to ask for it. When delivering bad news, such as sharing their low test scores, your student receives the feedback with a positive attitude and takes your advice seriously.

Positive student-teacher relationships don't happen by accident. They require you to make an effort to get to know all of your students. This may not occur overnight, however, making small positive gestures can go a long way toward making students feel safe and supported. Building connections with students who come from different racial or cultural backgrounds may require more intentionality to understand their needs and how they desire to be included and supported in the classroom. Reading diversity, equity, and inclusion books and materials and educating yourself on diverse cultures can make this process enjoyable for you!

Establishing Rapport

Strong connections are built through rapport. Rapport is a relationship that is built and nurtured through common interests. This is usually the foot in the door that allows for trust to form. Students are aware of the power imbalance that exists between you and them. It is clear to them that you are the authoritative figure and they are required to listen and follow your lead. Therefore, before they can learn to trust you, they must find commonalities that you share.

Establishing rapport is about highlighting what makes you the same. In a literal sense, you may share similar interests with some of your students which helps you connect. However, figuratively, you may have the same outlook or positive attitude about life. Laughing at your students' jokes or showing curiosity when they mention something interesting about their lives can also create the illusion of being similar. Both of you are engaged at the moment and bounce energy off each other.

Rapport can also be built by validating your students' thoughts and feelings. Instead of doing what many authoritative figures would do and instructing students on what to think and how to feel, you can show acceptance for their unique perspectives and seek to understand where they are coming from. You may not agree with everything they are saying, but showing validation makes them feel seen and heard. In other words, they feel comfortable sharing opposing views without fearing punishment.

Another way to build rapport is by asking questions. It is rare for teachers to take an interest in their students' lives beyond the classroom. However, getting to know them personally can help you establish a strong bond. Open-ended questions allow students to share as much as they feel comfortable with. They have control over what information they share and how deeply they open up. Be willing to also respond to questions when students seek to get to know you. Decide which aspects of your life you are comfortable sharing and steer conversations toward those topics. For example, topics related to your family may be off-limits, however, you consider your dog as your family and are open to sharing updates and stories on that topic.

Remember that building rapport is about finding common ground. Therefore, avoid topics or conversations that are conflictual. Keep the tone and content of your conversations positive and focused on identifying more ways to connect. Furthermore, building rapport involves showing interest in your students. Your conversations should focus more on understanding who they are rather than them seeking to understand who you are. During conversations, they should do more talking and you should do more listening. The advantage of listening is that you can learn more about your students' personalities, values, interests, social needs, and academic needs. They may also share stories about their personal lives and explain their family dynamics and living arrangements.

When your students are opening up, reassure them that what they share with you is considered private and confidential. Explain what this means using language they are likely to understand. While listening to their stories or opinions, remain non-judgmental and curious, so you can truly get a sense of who they are.

How to Build Rapport With Difficult Students?

Difficult students are those who display challenging behaviors that put a strain on your student-teacher relationship. They could be the students who talk over you, mock you, challenge your authority, throw tantrums, and refuse to follow instructions. Difficult students are used to receiving negative feedback, so they are not surprised when they are reprimanded. What surprises them is receiving compassion and understanding, despite not always behaving appropriately.

Students who behave poorly are likely to have low self-esteem and a harsh inner critical voice. They talk down to themselves and feel inadequate compared to other students. Building rapport with difficult students involves showing them that you are more similar than they think. Challenge their negative beliefs by showing kindness, praising their strengths, and being curious to learn more about them.

Building rapport with difficult students is as simple as taking the following steps:

Honor Students' Time, Interests, and Talents

Difficult students are sensitive to criticism and acts of dismissal or disrespect. Show them that you care by honoring their time and being organized. Thank them for coming to class and being ready to learn. Give the class a summary of the content you will cover and make the experience feel valuable. It is also important to honor your student's interests and talents by recognizing them. Instead of only asking questions about their interests and talents, find ways to incorporate them into the lessons. For example, you can base the themes of your content on students' diverse interests and talents, so they all get a moment to feel special.

Engage With Students on Their Level

Difficult students often feel misunderstood by others. Remind yourself of what it's like to be a student and the various pressures they might face. Think about the pressure to make friends, be accepted by the popular kids, or achieve high grades. When interacting with your students, anticipate potential withdrawal or avoidance. Be a little more patient and understanding of their hot and cold behaviors and respect their personal space. Make them feel in control of your interactions so that they can feel free to engage as much or as little as they want.

Accept Students' Differences

Your students are always watching to assess what type of teacher you are. Difficult students in particular will attempt to figure out whether they can be themselves around you or not. When you are overly critical of their behaviors, they may hide their authentic self. However, when you show acceptance of who they are while holding them accountable for their inappropriate behaviors, they may be inspired to modify their behaviors. Train yourself to see students separately from their behaviors. In other words, they may behave badly, but they are not bad people. Use positive reinforcement to highlight students' strengths, talents, and progress, and make that the center of your focus.

Fostering Independence and Empowerment

Another crucial way to build and nurture positive student-teacher relationships is to encourage autonomy and independence. While you want students to feel comfortable approaching you for help, you don't want them to be dependent on your assistance. The only way they can learn critical skills is by practicing them, over and over again. Of course, embracing change and discomfort is not easy, especially for students with ADHD, who prefer predictable routines and structures. Their natural instinct when feeling confused could be to approach your desk rather than attempt to solve the problem on their own.

Once again, scaffolding is the best approach to teaching your students how to think for themselves and work independently. Here are some strategies that you can implement in the classroom:

Provide Choices

Instead of making decisions on behalf of students, present two choices and allow them to pick the best option. Providing choices increases student motivation and makes them feel responsible for their learning. They feel in charge of their time and learning behaviors, which promotes good habits.

Set Clear Performance Standards

Make your performance standards clear from the beginning. State what type of work you will accept and won't accept. For example, you may not accept homework assignments that are torn, scrunched up, or have stains. When students understand the standards they need to uphold, they can push themselves to work more diligently.

Encourage Self-Assessments

Teach students how to review their work and assess progress. Attach performance checklists with assignments that can help them keep track of their progress. You can also introduce students to the practice of journaling. Whenever they feel proud of themselves, worried about school, or planning for an upcoming test, remind them to journal about their thoughts and feelings.

Encourage Brainstorming Solutions

Introduce students to mind maps and show them how to brainstorm possible solutions to challenges. Creative problem-solving is a skill that they will need throughout their lives. By cultivating this skill at the school level, they can reduce stress, build resilience, and strengthen their executive functioning. Establish a rule that students need to think about five possible solutions to their problems before approaching you for help.

Group Activity: Classroom Community Building

Lead a brainstorming session with other teachers and come up with ideas for cultivating a collaborative classroom environment. Share strategies for supporting at-risk students, being inclusive of students from diverse backgrounds, and fostering mutual respect among peers and between students and teachers.

Individual Activity: Get to Know Your Students

Create a monthly plan on how you are going to build rapport and engage with different students in the class. Include SMART goals that can drive your efforts on a daily and weekly basis. Review your progress at the end of the month.

The student-teacher relationship is a delicate one that can be strengthened through building rapport, trust, and independence. Use classroom interactions to connect with your students and get to know them better. Show acceptance and understanding to difficult students to challenge the negative beliefs they may hold about themselves. The next chapter will explore positive discipline strategies that work on students with ADHD.

Chapter 12:

Positive Discipline Strategies for Students With ADHD

ADHD is a challenge, not a curse. Find your strengths and let them shine. –Jackie McShannon

Understanding Positive Discipline

When students behave inappropriately in the classroom, to the extent that their behaviors affect the educator and other students, they need to be disciplined. There is a difference between discipline and punishment. Discipline refers to training or coaching students on the best actions to take or how to follow the rules.

Punishment refers to using force or aggression to control students' behaviors. In the short term, both discipline and punishment seem effective in correcting students' behaviors. However, in the long term, discipline leads to greater self-control and confidence while punishment leads to poor self-regulation and low self-esteem.

Students need to be told when their behaviors are not conducive to the learning environment and given the tools and responsibility to adjust their behaviors on their own. Positive discipline focuses on teaching students how to make good choices and manage their own behaviors. This is done in a non-aggressive and respectful way.

Part of your role as an educator is to protect and uphold your students' human and educational rights. For instance, it is their right to feel safe in the classroom, have equal access to learning opportunities, and express their thoughts and opinions without fear of punishment. Positive discipline allows you to mentor and work with your students, not against them. It involves building on their strengths and helping them improve on their weaknesses.

Positive discipline should not be confused with passivity or allowing students to do whatever they please. Classroom rules and standards are taught and reinforced to set reasonable expectations for students. They are encouraged to follow these rules and standards and will face appropriate consequences when they don't. Positive discipline is a proactive long-term approach to addressing challenging behaviors while fostering trust and cooperation.

The ABCs of Behavior

Positive discipline teaches educators how to respond rather than react to challenging behaviors in the classroom. One of the ways it does this is by emphasizing observation before taking action. The ABC data collection format is an effective method that you can use to make your observations and assess what is happening before deciding on a reasonable course of action.

ABC stands for antecedent, behavior, and consequence. The ABC data format requires you to zoom out of the problem and consider the situational factors that could be affecting the student's behavior. This requires spending enough time collecting information and going through the steps to gain deeper insight. Here is a breakdown of each step:

Antecedent: What Happened Before?

Behaviors don't occur without a cause. In many cases, they are promoted by a thought, emotion, impulse, or motivation. When a student behaves inappropriately, investigate what might have happened before the behavior occurred. What could have triggered them? What words were spoken? How were they feeling?

Behavior: What Is Happening?

Record the behavior that is taking place. Consider whether this behavior is an ongoing pattern or a once-off. If the student has performed this behavior before, notice whether they are repeating the same pattern. For example, when throwing a tantrum, are they yelling and spinning in circles on the floor?

When saying hurtful words, do they repeat the same words, and toward the same people?

Consequence: What Actions or Responses Followed?

Observe how the student behaves immediately after performing the behavior. Look at their facial expressions and body language to understand what they might be feeling. Do they show signs of being pleased with themselves? Do they act confused and withdrawn? You may also want to assess how you typically respond to the student during those moments. For instance, are you quick to reprimand them? Do you attempt to calm them down?

From the data collected using the ABC data format, you may be able to assess the root issue (or issues) that are negatively impacting your students' behaviors. Some of the questions to explore include:

- Could the student be experiencing difficulty understanding the learning material or learning approach?

- Could the student be lacking focus or motivation?

- Could the student's behaviors be a reflection of difficulties with peers or other school-related problems?

- Could the student's behaviors be a reflection of personal challenges at home?

- Could the student's behavior be a reflection of broader socio-economic issues that affect their ability to focus or learn in the classroom?

- Could the student's behavior be a reflection of underlying health issues or medical conditions?

The ABC data collection format promotes reflection and empathy toward students' behaviors so that the right approach can be taken to correct them. Remember that positive discipline is about training students to make good choices. If they aren't, it's important to understand what might be stopping them.

Positive Discipline Strategies in the Classroom

To encourage students to make the right choices, create a classroom environment that is conducive to the behaviors you wish to see. Implement positive discipline strategies as preventative measures to guide students' attitudes and behaviors. Here are a few ways that you can do this.

Establish a Classroom Code of Conduct

The classroom code of conduct outlines expectations that educators have for students as well as expectations that students have of educators. Both sets of rules should be created as a team by the entire class. All students should be allowed to voice their suggestions, and the best 4-8 rules will be chosen through a voting system.

The classroom code of conduct should focus on expected student and teacher behaviors. This means that after the code of conduct has been written and posted somewhere in the classroom, both you and your students will have new standards to live up to. Avoid creating too many rules that are difficult to remember and enforce. Choose only a few rules that students won't forget.

Examples of student rules include:

- We must arrive on time for our lesson.

- We must greet our teacher when entering the classroom.

- We must raise our hands when we want to speak.

- We must keep our desks tidy and throw papers in the trash.

- We must do our best to complete our homework.

Examples of teacher rules include:

- I must be cheerful and friendly toward my students.

- I must do my best to make lessons fun for students.

- I must be patient with my students when they don't understand instructions.

- I must treat all students equally and not show any favoritism.

- I must praise my students for good work and encourage them to succeed.

The code of conduct should be placed in a visible area on a large poster so that students can walk past and read over the expectations. During classroom discussions, refer back to the code of conduct and remind students of the agreement you made together. You can also paste a copy of the code of conduct on students' homework diaries and send a copy to their parents to inform them of the type of behaviors you expect from their children.

Constructive Discipline in Four Steps

Have you ever wondered how to get students to cooperate without raising your voice, making threats, or issuing immediate consequences? Constructive discipline teaches you how to stand in your authority while compassionately coaching students on how to behave appropriately.

Try these four steps the next time you need to address challenging behavior in the classroom:

Step 1: Describe the Appropriate Behavior

When you notice a student or group of students misbehaving, make a general announcement to the whole class and describe the appropriate behavior. This allows students to practice self-monitoring and adjust their behaviors accordingly.

Example: "Let's raise our hands instead of shouting out answers, please."

Step 2: Provide Reasons

Explain to students why it is important for them to perform the expected behavior. Use simple language so that they understand the significance of what you are telling them to do. Show them the value of modifying their behavior.

Example: "When we raise our hands, we get to hear everybody's thoughts and learn from each other."

Step 3: Ask Students to Acknowledge Appropriate Behavior

After students have successfully followed the instructions and modified their behaviors, take a moment to reflect on the difference between inappropriate and appropriate behavior. Get them to acknowledge the positive experience of behaving properly.

Example: "Can you see how much we were able to learn by raising our hands and allowing everybody to speak?"

Step 4: Reinforce the Appropriate Behavior

Naturally, students will forget the appropriate behavior and go back to doing what they had done before. Instead of getting upset, give social recognition and attention to the appropriate and ignore the inappropriate behavior. This reinforces the expectation you had set from the beginning.

Example: Do not acknowledge or engage with students who shout out answers. Look for students who have their hands up, nod your head, give a warm smile, and prompt them to speak. When the students who had previously shouted out answers decide to raise their hands, reward them with the same warmth and recognition.

Find Positive Distractions

Addressing every challenging behavior in the classroom can be counterproductive because it draws attention to bad choices instead of good choices. Some students deliberately misbehave as a way to disrupt the class and seek attention. Unless the behavior is threatening or seriously disruptive, choose to ignore it. Instead, turn the student's attention toward the desired behavior.

For example, if you are giving instructions and notice two students talking to each other, you can slowly start walking toward them. As you get closer, they are likely to end the conversation and pay attention. If you have students in your class who like to doodle, fidget, or lose focus easily, stand near them while giving instructions to show them that you are keeping a close watch on their behaviors.

Attention-seeking students will attempt to disrupt the class by making inappropriate jokes or distracting other students. Realize that what they need is a little bit of attention from you to settle down. While giving instructions, you can naturally insert their name to show recognition and get their attention. You could also ask them questions to provide an opportunity to speak or assign them a classroom task like handing out papers.

Setting Classroom Boundaries and Consequences

Classroom boundaries are the limits that you establish to guide positive behaviors. They express your standards and behaviors that you cannot tolerate. Healthy student-teacher relationships have boundaries that keep both students and teachers safe, satisfied, and comfortable in the classroom.

Fortunately, schools and districts already impose boundaries to guide student-teacher relationships, classroom conduct, and peer relationships. However, there could be certain boundaries that you have identified as being important in your diverse classroom that have not been noted by your school or district. You can create these additional boundaries for your students and include them as part of a set of expectations in your classroom.

Here are some tips for setting classroom boundaries:

- Reflect on your values and behaviors that would make you feel comfortable teaching your students. Consider your physical, mental, and emotional needs from students and how you can articulate these as boundaries.

- Introduce boundaries early in the school term or as soon as the need for them becomes apparent. Don't allow negative behavior to continue without proper boundaries being put in place.

- Outline the consequences of not adhering to the boundaries and provide scenarios of when boundary violations might occur. The aim of consequences is not to intimidate or threaten students but to show the importance of making good choices.

- There are special occasions when you may need to compromise on your boundaries. For instance, a student may be acting strange because of recently experiencing a traumatic incident. Their behavior is a sign of distress and urgent interventions and appropriate support need to be given to the student.

Two types of consequences can be established with boundaries: natural consequences and logical consequences. Natural consequences allow for cause and effect to take place without stepping in. For example, the natural consequence for not submitting an assignment is not being graded (i.e. getting zero for the assignment). You don't need to send reminders or make threats, just simply allow cause and effect to play out.

Logical consequences require strategy and empathy. Essentially, you need to decide on the best way to convey the importance of following rules while discouraging improper behaviors. Logical consequences are not harsh or punitive. They offer students an opportunity to reflect on their behaviors and self-correct. When establishing logical consequences, adopt the following three-tier approach:

- Tier 1: Issue a verbal warning and communicate the boundary.

- Tier 2: Repeat the boundary and state the consequences of continued violations.

- Tier 3: Issue the consequence without giving any warnings.

For example, when a student is seriously disrupting the class, issue a verbal warning and communicate a boundary. Say to them, "Josh, I don't like how you are choosing to behave. We do not distract other students when they are working."

If the student continues to perform the same behavior, repeat the boundary and state the consequence. For this particular violation, you would need a logical consequence. You might say to them, "Josh, this is the second time I am telling you to stop distracting other students. Your behavior is unacceptable. The next time you choose to behave this way, I will move you to the front of the class." If the student continues to make the wrong choice, despite being told the consequences, the next step is to take action and issue the consequence without warning. Create space in the front of the class and instruct them to move seats.

Group Activity: Boundary Reinforcement

Go around the table and discuss real-life behavioral issues that you have experienced in your classrooms. Mention how you addressed these issues and what you would have done differently. Assess whether you had clear and firm boundaries and effective consequences.

Individual Activity: Focus on Your ABCs

Refer back to the ABC data collection format mentioned in the chapter and recall a recent experience of challenging behavior in your classroom. Go through the steps and collect as much information as you can about the problem. Thereafter, ask yourself questions to gain a deeper understanding of the student's experience.

Positive discipline is not the same as punishment. When you are punishing students, you are forcefully seeking to control their behaviors. However, when you are disciplining students you are training them to make better choices and develop self-control. There are different ways to carry out positive discipline in the classroom. What's important to remember is to empathize with your students and always seek to help them do better.

We have now completed the third part of the book which explored ADHD-friendly communication strategies in the classroom. Let's proceed to the fourth and final part of the book which offers practical strategies for managing ADHD in elementary school, middle school, and high school.

PART 4:

Creating a Supportive Classroom Environment for Students With ADHD

Chapter 13:

ADHD-Friendly Strategies for Elementary School

I prefer to distinguish ADD as attention abundance disorder. Everything is just so interesting, remarkably at the same time. —Frank Coppola

Classroom Setup and Organization

At the elementary school level, students with ADHD may have less control over their inattention, hyperactivity, and impulsivity. They will need extra guidance and reinforcement to carry out instructions, remember the rules, and redirect their attention to schoolwork.

Create a Learning-Friendly Classroom

When students enter the classroom, they must be reminded that they are there to learn. Besides giving clear and concise instructions, you can rearrange your classroom to create an environment conducive to learning.

Be intentional about how you section your spaces and position the furniture. Students with ADHD need free space to get up and move around. The arrangements of the desks should also create a learning-friendly atmosphere. The table below provides suggestions on different layouts that may work in your classroom:

Seating arrangement	Advantages	Works best in these situations
Clusters of four to five desks.	The teacher and students can circulate more freely around the classroom.	Younger students who need more support and instruction. Supports collaboration and group projects. Hands-on creative tasks that require the sharing of materials.
U-shaped desk design with the teacher at the front.	Students have an interrupted view of the teacher and the whiteboard. Promotes a	Encourages students to pay attention to the teacher. Students are motivated to engage in classroom

Seating arrangement	Advantages	Works best in these situations
	collaborative classroom culture and fosters peer relationships.	discussions.
Two students sitting next to each other (i.e. two desks placed together)	Students can work independently and in pairs. The teacher and students can circulate freely around the classroom.	Students are encouraged to work in groups and seek support from each other.

Having designated areas for certain activities is another great way of helping students direct their focus on the important tasks at hand. For example, you can create playing, relaxing, and learning areas. Direct students to these areas during different parts of the day, so that they get accustomed to making smooth transitions. You can also use timers to help students keep track of how much time they get to spend in each area.

Students with ADHD need support to stay organized and keep their workspaces tidy. Allocate time for cleaning up after tasks and get the whole class involved. Before students leave, ask them to complete a checklist to ensure they have packed their belongings and picked up litter. Purchase storage bins, coat hooks, and stackable containers where students can store their personal belongings.

Social-Emotional Learning Integration

Social-emotional learning (SEL), commonly offered using the Collaborative for Academic, Social and Emotional Learning (CASEL) framework, seeks to make social and emotional learning an integral part of the learning process (Massachusetts Department of Elementary and Secondary Education, n.d.). Equity and inclusivity of students with diverse needs are at the forefront of teaching skills and knowledge that can help students develop healthy identities, regulate their emotions, cultivate empathy, and build supportive peer relationships.

SEL programs teach and reinforce five competencies at various stages of childhood development and across cultural contexts. The purpose of teaching these five competencies is to help students become aware of what is expected of them to build successful relationships, perform well at school, and make a meaningful contribution to their communities.

Here are the five competencies and examples of how you can teach them in your classroom:

Self-Awareness

Self-awareness is the recognition of one's thoughts and emotions and how they impact others or influence behaviors in different contexts. High self-awareness allows students to see both their strengths and weaknesses, and modify their behaviors to enhance learning and improve the quality of interactions with others.

These practices can help students develop self-awareness:

- teach students the difference between personal and social identities

- help students identify their personal, academic, linguistic, and cultural assets

- help students identify, describe, and label their emotions

- show students the connection between thoughts, emotions, and behaviors

- reinforce a growth mindset and develop a sense of purpose

Self-Management

For students to succeed at school, at home, and in other social spaces, they need to learn how to manage their thoughts, emotions, and behaviors effectively. Moreover, students need to be aware of appropriate behaviors in different social contexts.

Here are practices to teach self-management:

- teach students self-monitoring skills

- teach students appropriate stress management techniques

- show students how to set personal, social, and academic goals

- encourage students to take initiative and be curious about solving problems

- introduce students to smart planning and organizational skills

Social Awareness

To thrive in the classroom environment, students need to be mindful of others. Social awareness teaches them how to empathize with the experiences of other students (particularly those from different social or cultural backgrounds) and embrace broader perspectives.

These practices are great ways to drive social awareness in your classroom:

- encourage students to consider alternative perspectives

- teach students how to show concern for other people's feelings

- teach students how to recognize the situational demands of the classroom

- communicate classroom rules and hold students accountable to them

- help students learn how to practice gratitude and appreciation

Relationship Skills

Positive peer relationships are an essential component of student success. Students with ADHD may have challenges relating to others in healthy and appropriate ways, thus teaching relationship skills can provide necessary training and reinforcement.

Here are effective practices for teaching students relationship skills:

- show students how to communicate thoughts and emotions in healthy ways

- create opportunities for students to collaborate on tasks and projects

- encourage students to solve problems collectively

- promote compassion as a value in your classroom

- teach students how to ask for help or support when they need it

Responsible Decision-Making

Part of raising independent and responsible students involves teaching them how to make good choices. Responsible decision-making boosts students' confidence in themselves to make constructive decisions about their behaviors and evaluate the benefits and consequences of their actions.

These practices can help your students become responsible decision-makers:

- teach your students how to adopt a curious and open mindset

- allow students to brainstorm solutions to personal and social problems

- enforce consequences when boundaries are violated to promote reflection

- provide students with two choices and let them choose the best option

- assign students jobs around the classroom to promote personal responsibility

Behavior Management Strategies

It is normal for students at elementary age to break rules, make mistakes, and have difficulty regulating their thoughts and emotions. There are several ways to prevent and address challenging behaviors without causing disruptions to your classroom activities. Consider the following ADHD-friendly behavior management strategies:

Focus on the Positives

Draw your attention to the progress that your students are making and the desirable behaviors that they perform in the classroom. For every negative behavior that you identify in a student, challenge yourself to identify five positive behaviors before the end of the day, and offer praise and recognition. Students with ADHD need to hear what they are good at more often than they hear what they have done wrong to motivate positive behaviors.

Set a Good Example

Model the positive behaviors that you want to see in the classroom. For instance, if you want high energy in the mornings, start the day with high energy. If you want students to use good manners, show good manners toward them. If you want students to work as a team and enjoy collaboration, set a good example by building strong connections with each of them. Set the tone for social interactions in the classroom by demonstrating expected behaviors.

Countdown Technique

When students are misbehaving, let them know that you are going to countdown from 10 and when you reach 1, you expect them to follow the given instructions. Reinforce the technique by pausing in silence for a few seconds before continuing with your lesson. If they have not modified their behaviors after reaching 1, proceed to communicate a boundary and possible consequences.

Card System

Keep a set of red and yellow cards in the classroom. When a student goes against the rules or behaves inappropriately, issue a warning by handing out a yellow card. Place the card on their desk and explain the wrong choice they made. When the same student misbehaves again, issue a red card. The red card should come with a firm boundary and possible consequences for repeating behavior once more.

Rewards

Create a large reward chart to encourage students to modify their behaviors. Hand out stickers or tokens every time students commit desirable behaviors like completing classwork, working quietly, raising hands to speak, and so on. Provide a tangible reward when students have collected 10 stickers or tokens. The reward could be a certificate, coloring pencils, or a small toy.

Parent Support and Involvement

Parent engagement is crucial for the success of elementary students with ADHD. Since the students are still very young and going through several developmental changes, teachers and parents need to work together to identify challenges early on and provide necessary support.

Parents are often busy and may not always be reachable. However, you can be proactive about initiating communication and making sure that they stay informed about the progress of their children. Take into consideration the language and cultural differences between you. In multicultural schools, it is common to find families who are not native English speakers or may come from different religious or cultural backgrounds. Without being mindful of these differences, you may unintentionally approach parents in a manner they see as inappropriate.

Strike a balance between too little and too much parent involvement. Parents have placed their children in your trusted care and are comfortable allowing you to take the lead in deciding what is best for their children's education. While it is expected for parents to help children with school projects and read to them several times a week, they may not appreciate being given additional tasks that can be done in the classroom. If there are some really cool exercises that you believe students should be doing at home, present them as suggestions rather than requests, and give parents the choice.

Even when parents are not communicative with you, make an effort to consistently communicate with them. Find the best channels of communication for sending bulk and general announcements and personal student-related comments and feedback. Once again, you don't need to communicate everything with parents, such as your lesson plans. However, some information must be communicated, such as inappropriate behavior at school, classroom rules and code of conduct, disciplinary procedures, upcoming events and deadlines, referrals for special education services, and student performance reviews.

Lastly, be open to listening to parents' needs and expectations for their children. Find professional and proactive ways to address their concerns, calm their fears, and stay updated on the progress of their children. Parents of students with ADHD may need emotional support and guidance on how to navigate their children's disorder. Provide them with as much information as you can and refer them to the relevant experts who can offer assistance.

We have gone through specific strategies that are helpful for elementary school students with ADHD. In the next chapter, we will explore strategies that work best for middle school students with ADHD.

Chapter 14:

ADHD-Friendly Strategies for Middle School

With the disorganization, procrastination, inability to focus, and all the other bad things that come with ADHD, there also comes creativity and the ability to take risks. –David Neeleman

Fostering Self-Directed Learning

One of the main objectives of middle school is to equip students with the necessary skills and tools to work independently. This is an essential skill that they need to learn and master before they transition to high school. Due to executive function impairments, students with ADHD may have difficulty completing tasks and assignments independently. They may depend on your continuous instructions, reminders, and encouragement to get work done.

Fostering self-directed learning is about gradually letting go of your students' hands until they feel confident to take full control of their learning. Of course, your support won't be taken away completely. You will still be on standby in case students have questions or need assistance from you. Below are some of the ways that you can introduce self-directed learning to your students:

Encourage Students to Set Learning Goals

Learning requires active engagement. It isn't enough for students to sit back and listen to you speak without understanding how to apply and manipulate the information. Setting learning goals enables students to reflect on what they hope to achieve from lessons and how they see themselves improving skills and knowledge.

Have one-on-one sessions with your students and collaborate on 2-3 learning goals for the term. The goals should be based on areas that students need to work on. Have them lead the goal-setting session by writing down their goals using the SMART goal-setting framework. Offer guidance and suggestions when they look confused. Students should also come up with 2-3 ways that they will hold themselves accountable. Decide how often you will meet to review progress and discuss goals.

Teach Critical Thinking Skills

As students get older, they have to deal with increased demands and expectations. All of this can become overwhelming when students lack critical thinking skills. Critical thinking requires an awareness of oneself and one's surroundings, and deciding the best actions to take in different contexts. You can teach students how to think critically by introducing them to the 5 Ws:

- Who?

- What?

- Where?

- When?

- What?

Whenever your students are faced with a personal, social, or academic problem, encourage them to go through the 5Ws and gain a better understanding of their situation. After going through these five questions, ask them to brainstorm five workable solutions. Critical thinking allows students to expand their thinking capacity so that they can discover new and creative ways of solving problems.

Create Opportunities for Self-Evaluations

Students become unmotivated or lose interest in learning when they cannot measure their progress. To correct their mistakes and work harder, they need to reflect on past learning outcomes and assess what they can do differently. Self-evaluation processes allow students to reflect on their work and seek feedback. For instance, after receiving marked assignments, ask students to journal about what they did well and what they can improve next time. Here are some questions they can ask themselves:

- What did I learn from this assignment?

- What do I still not understand?

- What did I forget to do when completing the assignment?

- What do I need to work on to do better next time?

- What did I excel at and should continue to do?

Incorporate Technology Into Your Lessons

Students need to understand that you are not their only source of information. We are fortunate enough to live in a technological age that offers sophisticated methods for sourcing information and enhancing the learning experience. Incorporating technology into your lessons can be a fun way to promote self-directed learning. Students are required to tap into the wealth of information on student-friendly apps and websites and engage with learning material. Students with ADHD will love working with technology because of the stimulation it provides, as well as the entertainment factor. The more pleasure they find in their learning, the higher their engagement will be.

Implementing Universal Design for Learning

Universal Design for Learning (UDL) is an instructional approach to learning that was introduced in the early civil rights and special education legislation. The purpose of UDL is to create a learning environment where all students have equal access to education. Students with learning and developmental conditions often face challenges keeping up with the pace of mainstream school because of their unique reading, writing, and speaking challenges. UDL levels the playing field by using universal design principles to remove as many restrictions to learning and create an inclusive curriculum.

The best part about UDL is that all students benefit, not just students with ADHD. The three principles of UDL state that the curriculum should offer multiple, diverse, and flexible options to present learning materials and enhance engagement (Ralabate, 2023). Here are effective ways that you can integrate UDL into your lesson plans:

Assess Diverse Student Needs

The first thing to consider is that no student is the same. Every student has academic strengths and weaknesses that inform their learning needs and preferences. Get to understand the diverse needs of your students and their preferred learning styles. You may even want to consider what interests or entertains your students so that you can incorporate these themes into your lessons.

Evaluate Lesson Barriers

Take a broad look at your lesson plans and identify barriers that disadvantage some students. For example, you may have lessons that consist of mostly verbal instructions. Staying focused in these lessons can be a challenge for students with ADHD. You may also have lessons where critical or problem-solving skills are required. To keep up with the rest of the class during these lessons, students with ADHD may need additional support in the form of clear instructions, visual aids, demonstrations, and active participation. Adjust your lessons to provide support tools for students with learning difficulties.

Offer Multiple Means of Representation and Engagement

Think out of the box when deciding on how to represent information. Consider the fact that you have students in the class who learn best through written text, images, videos, audio, and active learning. It is not possible to incorporate all of these representations into single lessons. However, aim to include 2-3 different representations in each lesson. You are welcome to take a poll and ask students what types of representations they would like to see more of. There are many ways to assess how engaged your students are with the class content. For instance, you can simply ask for their opinions, provide self-monitoring checklists after submitting assignments, or assess the levels of participation during classroom discussions.

Integrate Executive Function Support

We have touched on the importance of designing lessons that are inclusive and considerate of students' diverse learning needs. Students with ADHD will need extra support when completing coursework that incorporates executive functioning skills. To ensure that all students benefit from the additional support, adjust your lessons to include executive function support, such as reflection questions, visual charts, reminders, important tips, checklists, schedules, and detailed guidelines on how to perform the activity.

Strategies for Smoother Transitions

Students with ADHD struggle with classroom transitions because their brains cannot swiftly redirect focus from one activity to another. The process of transitioning can also be deeply uncomfortable, especially when students are hyperfocused on preferred tasks. Some transitions may require a change of behavior, which can also be difficult for students to accept. For example, during Math lessons, students may need to concentrate harder than they do in other subjects. Making this shift can feel overwhelming for students.

Teaching students how to manage transitions can improve their overall attitude and behavior in the classroom. They understand what is coming and how to mentally and emotionally prepare themselves for it. The following strategies will help you teach students how to navigate transitions successfully:

Use Timers

Users timers to cue students of upcoming transitions. Let them know how much time they have and alert them when they have 10 minutes, 5 minutes, and 2 minutes remaining. Preferably, use a visible timer that you can place at the front of the class. This teaches students to be mindful of how much time they have and to use their time constructively.

Have Movement Breaks

Instead of going straight into the next task, offer students a movement break. Let them stand up, stretch their legs, go to the restroom, and move around the classroom. Movement breaks give the mind a moment to breathe and reset. Students will feel refreshed when they head back to their seats.

Use Visual Reminders

Visual reminders are a great way to cue students for upcoming subjects on their timetables or upcoming tasks on their schedules and calendars. The visual reminders should be pasted or posted in a place where students can see them. For example, you can post the monthly calendar in a section of the classroom with high foot traffic or get your students to paste a copy of their timetables inside their homework diaries.

Explain the Purpose

Students may want to know why they need to stop doing one task and move on to another task. Have an explanation prepared to help them understand the reason for the transition. Instead of giving a vague response like "It's just what we have to do," give a response that can help them buy into the change. You might say, "I know you are enjoying writing your essay, but we need to practice reading as well so that you feel confident expressing your interesting thoughts!"

Define What "Finished" Looks Like

It can be upsetting for students with ADHD to abruptly stop what they are doing because they ran out of time or the school bell rang. Be clear about how much you expect for them to complete within a certain period. For example, if you have given students 10 minutes at the end of the class to start their homework, they are not likely to finish their homework in that timeframe. Thus, you might only expect them to complete the first activity before the bell rings. Set the expectations low so that all students, regardless of their speed can achieve them.

Use Visualization

When students are preparing for an upcoming task or assignment that makes them feel anxious, encourage them to visualize the step-by-step process of completing the task or assignment, from start to finish. For example, if students need to deliver prepared speeches, paint a picture of what they can expect on the day, how you would like them to stand and engage the class, and so on. Go through the worst-case scenarios like forgetting cue cards at home or freezing and not knowing what to say, and present solutions.

We have gone through practical classroom strategies that are useful for middle school students with ADHD. Let us now proceed to look at classroom strategies for managing ADHD at the high school level in the next chapter.

Chapter 15

ADHD-Friendly Strategies for High School

ADHD hasn't changed me...It is me. It's an undeniable and simple fact of who I am. —Tilly

Personalized Learning Plans

Research from the US Department of Education found that during the 2015-2016 period, only 84% of students graduated from high school (US Department of Education, 2017). There are over 500,000 students who dropout of school before completing high school, and many of them are at-risk students.

Students with ADHD fall under *at-risk students* because many of them fail to meet the minimal academic proficiencies in key subjects or may display challenging behaviors in the classroom that lead to frequent disciplinary procedures and expulsions, in extreme cases.

One of the strategies put forward by the US Department of Education was for schools and districts to consider developing personalized learning plans for at-risk students. Personalized learning is a teaching model that seeks to tailor learning to the specific needs, skills, and interests of students. The pace and style of learning are different from the normal curriculum provided by schools, however, the plans are designed to ensure that at-risk students stay on track to meet the requirements to proceed to the next grade.

Teachers work together with targeted students to create personalized learning plans. They agree on realistic short- and long-term and continuously evaluate performance to make sure that students are meeting the academic standards. It's important to note that while personalized learning plans sound similar to special education programs, they do not replace seeking specialized interventions. Students don't need to be living with a medical condition to qualify for personalized learning. Teachers simply make accommodations and offer individualized support.

Even though personalized learning plans were developed for at-risk students, they can benefit all students. Schools wishing to adopt a personalized learning model can decide what approach they want to take. Here are the four common ways schools implement personalized learning:

Using Student Profiles and Records

Schools can use student profiles and records to collect and analyze student needs, performance, and challenges. This information informs the type of personal support that teachers offer students. To get the most out of these records, schools need to regularly update student information and create profiles that provide rich data that you wouldn't find on a report card. For example, student profiles could include medical history, family history, progress reports, behavior issues, and so on.

Using Personalized Learning Paths

Some schools go the extra mile to create personalized learning paths for each student based on set goals and progress. For example, a school might update their student's weekly or monthly schedule based on the most recent performance report. Another school might customize a student's schedule based on their key strengths and interests. What's unique about this model is that no student's schedule will look the same, however, there is a combination of group work, independent work, and one-on-one tutoring.

Using Competency-Based Progression

Schools that use competency-based progression regularly monitor students' progress toward outlined goals. Instead of students focusing on every skill or every subject, they are given specific competencies to focus on and master. Students receive specialized support to develop skills, mindsets, and knowledge. Once they have achieved their goals, they are required to demonstrate their mastery in a practical way. For example, a student might work with their art teacher to set up a showcase of their work.

Using Flexible Learning Environments

Some schools assess student needs and adapt the learning environment to match their preferred learning styles. The type of adjustments made can range from rearranging the classroom layout to modifying the curriculum. Teachers may also receive additional training to help them learn new skills and transform their approach to giving instructions and providing support to students.

Not many schools have adopted personalized learning, which means we don't have a lot of data evaluating the effectiveness of this teaching approach. Nevertheless, personalized learning has the potential to create more inclusive schools and classrooms where students with learning differences can learn at their own pace while meeting academic standards and graduating with their peers.

Study Skills and Test-Taking Strategies

The pressure to meet academic standards becomes intense as students transition into high school. At the back of their minds, they wonder whether they are doing enough to advance to the next grade. Some students may have dreams of going to college and feel an overwhelming pressure to excel academically.

To compensate for their learning challenges, students with ADHD will spend more time studying than their peers, but still, their grades won't reflect the amount of time and effort they have invested. Once again, this has to do with impaired executive functioning that makes tasks like planning, organizing, and memorizing information challenging.

Study skills and strategies can help students improve their focus, memory, planning, time management, and motivation.

They seek to simplify the way students process, categorize, and store information in their brains. These skills and strategies are not only useful in exam and assessment situations; they can also help students summarize classwork or process information quickly.

Here is a list of study skills and strategies that you can practice with your students:

Pomodoro Technique

Students with ADHD often struggle to concentrate on tasks for an extended period. The Pomodoro technique teaches students how to sustain concentration by focusing on small intervals and taking short breaks in between. Here are the instructions for carrying out the Pomodoro technique:

- Identify a task that you would like to focus on.

- Set a timer for 25 minutes and start the task.

- Focus solely on the task at hand and block out other distractions.

- When the time is complete, set a timer for 5 minutes, and take a break.

- After the break, decide on the next task to focus on and repeat the steps.

Students can decide how many Pomodoros they want to complete before taking an extended break. In general, they should aim to complete four Pomodoros, which would total an hour of complete focus.

Multiple Learning Methods

Not everyone can memorize information using parrot learning. It's important for students to explore various learning methods and choose a few that can help them process and store information efficiently. Note that subjects like math or accounting may require specific learning methods. However, general subjects that consist of a lot of written text can be revised using any of these methods:

Flashcards

Create or purchase a set of cards. Write down questions on one side of the cards and answers on the other. When studying, go through the cards, one-by-one, and read out the questions. Look away and attempt to answer the questions without referring to the correct responses written on the back of the cards. Flip over the cards and read the correct answers. Compare how closely your answers match the responses on the card.

Spaced Repetition

Instead of cramming large quantities of information at once, pick smaller sections to revise at intervals. For example, you might decide to divide a topic into three subtopics and spend each day revising a subtopic, over and over again. At the end of the three days, start the cycle again.

Retrieval Practice

Test how well you understand a concept by pulling out information from your memory. You can do this by completing past papers, creating tests for yourself, asking a friend to test your knowledge by asking subject questions, or using flashcards. Grade yourself like a teacher would in a real test situation and provide feedback.

Feynman Technique

The Feynman technique involves explaining complex ideas and concepts using simple everyday language, as though you were speaking to a friend or someone who didn't know anything about the subject. This is a great way to simplify information for yourself and reinforce learning.

Minimize Distractions

ADHD creates attention difficulties that make focusing on tasks tough. Since students with ADHD are more susceptible to distractions, they must make a conscious effort to remove anything that might cause them. Distractions refer to any stimuli that break focus. This could range from unwanted thoughts to sounds of cars driving past your house. Even though it is impossible to physically remove all distractions, there are ways to minimize them, such as:

- block out subtle noises in your room with a white noise machine

- wear a pair of noise-canceling headphones when studying

- remove stationery supplies and unnecessary textbooks from your study desk.

- put your phone on silent or consider placing it in another room.

- find a quiet time to study when there is minimal movement around the house.

When students are battling with worries or disturbing thoughts, encourage them to write down their thoughts on paper, then shifting the attention back to studying. After the study session, they can read over their thoughts and brainstorm ways to address the challenges.

Transition Planning and College Readiness

In the previous chapter, we discussed classroom transitions that occur on a daily basis. However, the transition from high school to college is a life-altering one that can cause an overwhelming fear for students with ADHD. Due to the challenges they have faced throughout their schooling, students with ADHD feel unprepared for the demands of college.

Some of these fears are warranted. For instance, not all college subject fields are accommodating to students with ADHD. Moreover, college lecturers may not avail themselves of support as much as high school teachers do. There are also some student accommodations that may not cater to students with special needs. Nevertheless, with the right amount of planning and preparation, students can find suitable fields of study and inclusive college institutions to attend.

Here is a college checklist that you can complete with students who are seeking to go to college:

Have You Done Your Research?

The most important step to prepare for college is to conduct research. The information you collect should focus on finding the right field of study that aligns with your interests and personality, as well as looking for institutions that provide special education services, counseling, treatments, and skills-based groups to students with ADHD.

Finding the right field of study requires self-assessments, such as taking online personality tests, consulting teachers, or answering a few questions about yourself, such as:

- What do you like to do on the weekends?

- What is your favorite subject?

- What are your interests and talents?

- What do you frequently Google in your spare time?

- What social causes matter to you?

College Success Skills

There are certain skills required to thrive in a college environment. Fortunately, many of these skills are taught and reinforced at school and home. However, it is still important to master them before going to college. College success skills include:

- problem-solving

- independence

- critical thinking

- innovation

- networking

- organization

- adaptability

- stress management

- emotional intelligence

- time management

- communication

To improve these skills, find ways to practice them at home, school, or during school breaks. Consider taking on more chores around the house, living on a budget, getting a summer internship, or volunteering at a local shelter. These activities reinforce important life skills that you will need in college, at the workplace, and beyond.

College is not a mandatory next step for students after high school. The college environment is not designed to accommodate every child's learning needs or purpose. Expose students to alternatives to college, such as enrolling in a college internship program (CIP), going to a vocational school, finding a job, or taking a gap year and doing volunteer work, tutoring, freelancing, or traveling the world.

Conclusion

Each one of us is different, but one thing that is true; Each one of us is wonderfully made, and so, my dear, are you!
–Donna Anello

Empowering Teachers to Support Students with ADHD

Teachers are the unsung heroes who mentor the leaders of tomorrow. Without the tireless efforts that you make every day to help students build their thinking capacities, our world would be a different place.

Students with ADHD bring so much vibrancy to the classroom. However, they need support to channel that energy toward learning and building positive peer relationships. With your dedication to understanding how students with ADHD think, feel, and behave at school, you can provide the type of inclusive and supportive environment they need to thrive.

This book is a comprehensive resource that you can turn to whenever you need a refresher on how to manage ADHD behaviors in the classroom. You have gained a library of skills and strategies to identify ADHD in your classroom, carry out suitable interventions, and adapt your teaching approach to students with inattentiveness, hyperactivity, and a combination of both.

As you may know, communication and collaboration are key to providing meaningful support to students with ADHD. You must work as a team with other educators, parents, medical doctors, school districts, and therapists, who can provide specialized assistance to at-risk students.

Communication and collaboration are two values that you can also promote in your classroom. Students are watching your behaviors to decide on how they should relate to you and their peers. Model positive communication skills, teamwork, and empathy to create a safe and accepting space for all students—regardless of their age, race, gender, culture, religion, or disability—to feel welcomed.

Reflecting on the Journey

You have successfully read through 15 chapters filled with evidence-based strategies on how to manage ADHD in the classroom. Along the way, you have taken breaks to complete the group and individual activities to consolidate your learning. The only thing left to do now is to go back to your classroom and put these strategies into practice. Feel free to refer back to the book whenever you need encouragement.

Remember that no student is the same and what works for one may not work for someone else. Be willing to test various strategies and modify lessons until you find a teaching formula that accommodates the diverse needs of your students. Stay informed on trends and developments in the educational space and continue to meet with your community of educators. Your continued investment in your professional development will positively impact your teaching experience.

If you have found this guide beneficial, please leave a comment on the Amazon page and share your experience. I would love to hear back from you!

About the Author

Richard Bass is a well-established author with extensive knowledge and background on children's disabilities. Richard has also experienced first-hand many children and teens who deal with depression and anxiety. He enjoys researching techniques and ideas to serve students better, as well as guiding parents on how to understand and lead their children to success.

Richard wants to share his experience, research, and practices through his writing as it has proven successful for many parents and students.

Richard feels there is a need for parents and others around the child to fully understand the disability or the mental health of the child. He hopes that with his writing people will be more understanding of children who suffer from these issues.

Richard Bass has been in education for over a decade and holds a bachelor's and master's degree in education, as well as several certifications, including Special Education K-12 and Educational Administration.

Whenever Richard is not working, reading, or writing he likes to travel with his family to learn about different cultures and get ideas from all around about the upbringing of children especially those with disabilities. Richard also researches and learns about different educational systems around the world.

He participates in several online groups where parents, educators, doctors, and psychologists share their success with children with disabilities. Richard is in the process of growing a Facebook group where further discussion about his books and techniques could take place. Apart from online groups, he has also attended training regarding the upbringing of students with disabilities and has also led training in this area.

A Message from the Author

If you enjoyed the book and are interested on further updates or just a place to share your thoughts with other readers or myself, please join my Facebook group by scanning below!

If you would be interested on receiving a FREE Planner for kids PDF version, by signing up you will also receive exclusive notifications to when new content is released and will be able to receive it at a promotional price. Scan below to sign up!

Scan below to check out my content on You Tube and learn more about Neurodiversity!

References

ADDA Editorial Team. (2023, August 30). *How to study efficiently with ADHD: 7 tips to boost focus & motivation*. Attention Deficit Disorder Association. https://add.org/tips-for-studying-with-adhd/

ADDitude Editors. (2021, April 27). *Managing transitions for children with ADHD*. Additude Mag. https://www.additudemag.com/managing-transitions-adhd-children/

ADDitude Editors. (2024, March 12). *Easily distracted at school? Focus tips for children with ADHD*. Additude Mag. https://www.additudemag.com/end-distractibility-improving-adhd-focus-at-home-and-school/

ADHD Editorial Board. (2022, October 28). *Following every direction, every time*. Additude Mag. https://www.additudemag.com/following-directions/

Alder, S. L. (2022, April 15). *ADHD quotes about the neurodivergent way of paying attention*. Everyday Power. https://everydaypower.com/adhd-quotes/

American Psychological Association. (2020). *Students experiencing inattention and distractibility*. American Psychological Association. https://www.apa.org/ed/schools/primer/inattention

American Psychological Association. (2024). *Improving students' relationships with teachers to provide essential supports for learning*. American Psychological Association. https://www.apa.org/education-career/k12/relationships

Anello, D. (2023, September 9). *Be Inspired: 30 quotes about autism, ADHD and parenting*. Autism and ADHD Connection.

https://autismadhdconnection.com/be-inspired-30-quotes-about-autism-adhd-and-parenting/

Bachrach, S. (2016). *Individualized education programs (ieps): Tips for teachers (for parents) - kidshealth.* KidsHealth. https://kidshealth.org/en/parents/iep-teachers.html

Barkley, R. (n.d.). *Russell A. Barkley quote.* Goodreads. Retrieved March 23, 2024, from https://www.goodreads.com/author/show/215511.Russell_A_Barkley

Ben-Aharon, A. (2020, November 12). *Six tips for adults to help children with ADHD and dyslexia.* Great Speech. https://greatspeech.com/6-ways-to-help-language-disorders-for-kids-with-adhd-dyslexia/

Carnegie Mellon University. (2003). *Problematic student behavior.* Carnegie Mellon University. https://www.cmu.edu/teaching/designteach/teach/problemstudent.html

Carpenter, L. (2016, February 1). *Four ways children can make friends.* Kids in Transition to School. https://kidsintransitiontoschool.org/4-ways-children-can-make-friends/

Centers for Disease Control and Prevention. (2020, October 5). *ADHD and school changes.* Centers for Disease Control and Prevention. https://www.cdc.gov/ncbddd/adhd/features/adhd-and-school-changes.html

Centers for Disease Control and Prevention. (2022a). *Symptoms and diagnosis of ADHD.* Centers for Disease Control and Prevention. https://www.cdc.gov/ncbddd/adhd/diagnosis.html

Centers for Disease Control and Prevention. (2022b, August 9). *Data and statistics about ADHD*. Centers for Disease Control and Prevention. https://www.cdc.gov/ncbddd/adhd/data.html

Coastal Carolina Community College. (2019). *Active learning/student engagement*. Coastal Carolina Community College. https://www.coastalcarolina.edu/faculty-staff/professional-development/instructional-resources/active-learning/

Copper, J. (2018, June 14). *S is for self-regulation: Lessons in ADHD emotional control from "sesame street."* ADDitude. https://www.additudemag.com/self-regulation-sesame-street-adhd-children/

Coppola, F. (2023, September 9). *Be Inspired: 30 quotes about autism, ADHD and parenting*. Autism and ADHD Connection. https://autismadhdconnection.com/be-inspired-30-quotes-about-autism-adhd-and-parenting/#google_vignette

DeSantis, M. (2022, August 17). *Three ways to give directions to help kids with ADHD*. Understood. https://www.understood.org/en/articles/3-ways-to-give-directions-to-help-kids-with-adhd

Edmentum. (n.d.). *Ten steps to creating personalized learning plans for students*. Edmentum. https://www.edmentum.com/articles/10-steps-to-creating-personalized-learning-plans/

Ekpezu, N. (2023, April 14). *The importance of confidentiality in school administration: How to handle sensitive information*. Nancy Ekpezu. https://www.nancyekpezu.com/blog/confidentialityinadministration

Emma. (2023). *Five secrets to classroom transitions that actually work*. TeachStarter. https://www.teachstarter.com/gb/blog/the-secret-to-effective-classroom-transitions-us/

Enfinger, C., & Murphy, J. (2016, November 28). *The high school study guide for teens with ADHD*. ADDitude Mag.

https://www.additudemag.com/slideshows/adhd-in-high-school/

Eredics, N. (2023). *Nine ways to teach social skills in your classroom.* Reading Rockets. https://www.readingrockets.org/topics/social-emotional-learning/articles/9-ways-teach-social-skills-your-classroom

Finn, A. J. (2022, April 15). *ADHD quotes about the neurodivergent way of paying attention.* Everyday Power. https://everydaypower.com/adhd-quotes/

Francis, J. (2022, December 7). *Nine examples of boundaries to implement in the classroom.* Alludo Learning. https://blog.alludolearning.com/classroom-boundaries

Gill, T., & Hosker, T. (2021, February 10). *How ADHD may be impacting your child's social skills and what you can do to help.* Foothills Academy. https://www.foothillsacademy.org/community/articles/adhd-social-skills

Green, R. (2024, February 18). *ADHD symptom spotlight: Lack of focus.* Verywell Mind. https://www.verywellmind.com/understanding-and-managing-lack-of-focus-in-adhd-5216984

Grizenko, N., Fortier, M.-E., Zadorozny, C., Thakur, G., Schmitz, N., Duval, R., & Joober, R. (2012). Maternal stress during pregnancy, ADHD symptomatology in children and genotype: Gene-Environment interaction. *Journal of the Canadian Academy of Child and Adolescent Psychiatry, 21*(1), 9–15. https://www.ncbi.nlm.nih.gov/pmc/articles/PMC3269259/

Hallowell, E. M. (2022a, April 15). *ADHD quotes about the neurodivergent way of paying attention.* Everyday Power. https://everydaypower.com/adhd-quotes/

Hallowell, E. M. (2022b, April 15). *ADHD quotes about the neurodivergent way of paying attention.* Everyday Power. https://everydaypower.com/adhd-quotes/

Hallowell, E. M. (2022c, April 15). *ADHD quotes about the neurodivergent way of paying attention.* Everyday Power. https://everydaypower.com/adhd-quotes/

Haraway, D. L. (2012). Monitoring students with ADHD within the RTI framework. *International Journal of Behavioral Consultation & Therapy, 13*(2). https://files.eric.ed.gov/fulltext/EJ1004993.pdf

Harvard University. (n.d.). *What is executive function? How executive functioning skills affect early development.* Center on the Developing Child at Harvard University; Harvard University. https://developingchild.harvard.edu/resources/what-is-executive-function-and-how-does-it-relate-to-child-development/

Institute of Teacher Aide Courses. (n.d.). *Building rapport in the classroom.* Institute of Teacher Aide Courses. https://www.itac.edu.au/resources/building-rapport

Johnson, B. (2018, October 10). *Working to grow students' trust and respect.* Edutopia. https://www.edutopia.org/article/working-grow-students-trust-and-respect/

Kaczegowicz, C. (2023, February 1). *Visual aids: A vital tool for students with ADHD.* Medium. https://medium.com/@ckaczeducation/visual-aids-a-vital-tool-for-students-with-adhd-bbf3a9eb5b25

Locke, J. (2022, April 15). *ADHD quotes about the neurodivergent way of paying attention.* Everyday Power. https://everydaypower.com/adhd-quotes/

Massachusetts Department of Elementary and Secondary Education. (n.d.). *Social and emotional learning in Massachusetts.* Department

of Education.
https://www.doe.mass.edu/sfs/sel/?section=sel#topics

McCombs, B. (2021). *Developing responsible and autonomous learners: A key to motivating students.* American Psychological Association.
https://www.apa.org/education-career/k12/learners

McCormick, S. (2023, January 25). *Seventeen ways to teach executive functioning skills in school.* EF Specialists.
https://www.efspecialists.com/post/17-ways-to-teach-executive-functioning-skills-in-school#viewer-6n2tg

McShannon, J. (n.d.). *Adhd quotes (81 quotes).* Goodreads.
https://www.goodreads.com/quotes/tag/adhd

Meador, D. (2019, July 1). *Basic strategies for providing structure in the classroom.* ThoughtCo.
https://www.thoughtco.com/strategies-for-structure-in-the-classroom-4169394

Miller, C. (2016, February 26). *What's ADHD (and what's not) in the classroom.* Child Mind Institute.
https://childmind.org/article/whats-adhd-and-whats-not-in-the-classroom/

Morin, A. (2022a). *Accommodations to help students with ADD and ADHD.* Understood.
https://www.understood.org/en/articles/classroom-accommodations-for-adhd

Morin, A. (2022b). *What is personalized learning.* Understood.
https://www.understood.org/en/articles/personalized-learning-what-you-need-to-know

National Institutes of Health. (2007, November 12). *Brain matures a few years late in ADHD, but follows normal pattern.* National Institutes of Health (NIH). https://www.nih.gov/news-events/news-releases/brain-matures-few-years-late-adhd-follows-normal-pattern

Neeleman, D. (2023, September 9). *Be Inspired: 30 quotes about autism, ADHD and parenting.* Autism and ADHD Connection. https://autismadhdconnection.com/be-inspired-30-quotes-about-autism-adhd-and-parenting/

Nerenberg, J. (2022, April 15). *ADHD quotes about the neurodivergent way of paying attention.* Everyday Power. https://everydaypower.com/adhd-quotes/

NHS. (2021, December 24). *Causes - attention deficit hyperactivity disorder (ADHD).* NHS. https://www.nhs.uk/conditions/attention-deficit-hyperactivity-disorder-adhd/causes/

NICHCY. (2011, March). *Categories of disabilities under IDEA.* Parent Center Hub. https://www.parentcenterhub.org/wp-content/uploads/repo_items/gr3.pdf

Nichols, H. (2023, July 28). *Inattentive ADHD: Symptoms, diagnosis, and treatment.* Www.medicalnewstoday.com. https://www.medicalnewstoday.com/articles/315359#symptoms-and-diagnosis

Patel, H. (2018, June 4). *The impact of ADHD on learning.* News Medical. https://www.news-medical.net/health/The-Impact-of-ADHD-on-Learning.aspx

PBIS Rewards. (2020, November 3). *The importance of teaching social skills.* PBIS Rewards. https://www.pbisrewards.com/blog/the-importance-of-teaching-social-skills/

Pratt, C., & Dubie, M. (n.d.). *Observing behavior using A-B-C data.* Indiana Resource Center for Autism. https://www.iidc.indiana.edu/irca/articles/observing-behavior-using-a-b-c-data.html

Ralabate, P. (2023). *Universal design for learning: Meeting the needs of all students | reading rockets.* Reading Rockets. https://www.readingrockets.org/topics/assistive-technology/articles/universal-design-learning-meeting-needs-all-students

ReachOut. (n.d.). *Helping students to form quality friendships.* ReachOut. https://schools.au.reachout.com/articles/helping-students-form-quality-friendships

Richardson, J. E. (2022, April 15). *ADHD quotes about the neurodivergent way of paying attention.* Everyday Power. https://everydaypower.com/adhd-quotes/

Robertshaw, S. (2023, October 11). *"How teachers can initiate and promote inclusive education."* ADDitude. https://www.additudemag.com/inclusive-education-learning-challenges-adhd/

Rose, L. T. (2022, April 15). *ADHD quotes about the neurodivergent way of paying attention.* Everyday Power. https://everydaypower.com/adhd-quotes/

Shingleton, E. (2023, February 2). *How to create an inclusive classroom: 12 tips for teachers.* PlanBee. https://planbee.com/blogs/news/how-to-create-an-inclusive-classroom-12-tips-for-teachers

Shurley, B. (n.d.). *How to cultivate executive functioning skills for students.* Branching Minds. https://www.branchingminds.com/blog/executive-functioning-skills-for-students-mtss

Sinclair, K. (2023, March 10). *What is the impact of ADHD on self-regulation?* EF Specialists. https://www.efspecialists.com/post/what-is-the-impact-of-adhd-on-self-regulation#viewer-ce9ag

Smith, M., & Segal, J. (2019). *Teaching students with ADHD.* HelpGuide. https://www.helpguide.org/articles/add-adhd/teaching-students-with-adhd-attention-deficit-disorder.htm

South African Department of Basic Education. (2012). Positive discipline and classroom management course reaDer school safety framework. In *Western Cape Education Online*. https://wcedonline.westerncape.gov.za/documents/Psycho-Social%20Support/Positive%20Behaviour%20Programme/PBP%20Resources%20for%20Teachers/positive_classroom_discipline_and_classroom_management_reader.pdf

Tartakovsky, M. (2021, September 24). *ADHD: When criticism and rejection hurts*. Psych Central. https://psychcentral.com/adhd/adults-with-adhd-when-youre-super-sensitive-to-rejection#why-it-happens

Thirteen types of students you see in every classroom. (2023, December 14). University of the People. https://www.uopeople.edu/blog/13-types-of-students-you-see-in-every-classroom/

Tilly. (2023, September 9). *Be Inspired: 30 quotes about autism, ADHD and parenting*. Autism and ADHD Connection. https://autismadhdconnection.com/be-inspired-30-quotes-about-autism-adhd-and-parenting/

Tyler, A. (2021, November 19). *The importance of praise in parenting a child with ADHD*. HappyNeuron Pro . https://news.happyneuronpro.com/the-importance-of-praise-in-parenting-a-child-with-adhd/

University of South Carolina. (n.d.). *Importance of providing meaningful student feedback*. University of South Carolina. https://sc.edu/about/offices_and_divisions/cte/teaching_resources/grading_assessment_toolbox/providing_meaningful_student_feedback/index.php

University of Washington. (n.d.). *Active learning*. University of Washington. https://teaching.washington.edu/engaging-students/active-learning/

University of Waterloo. (n.d.). *Self-Directed learning: A four-step process.* University of Waterloo. https://uwaterloo.ca/centre-for-teaching-excellence/catalogs/tip-sheets/self-directed-learning-four-step-process

US Department of Education. (2016). Know your rights: Students with ADHD. In *US Department of Education.* https://www2.ed.gov/about/offices/list/ocr/docs/dcl-know-rights-201607-504.pdf

US Department of Education. (2017). *Issue brief: Personalized learning plans.* https://www2.ed.gov/rschstat/eval/high-school/personalized-learning-plans.pdf

US Department of Education. (2023). *Individuals with disabilities education act.* US Department of Education. https://sites.ed.gov/idea/about-idea

Van Diest, R. (2022, April 15). *ADHD quotes about the neurodivergent way of paying attention.* Everyday Power. https://everydaypower.com/adhd-quotes/

Watermark Insights. (2023, September 7). *The importance of developing rapport with students.* Watermark Insights. https://www.watermarkinsights.com/resources/blog/the-importance-of-developing-rapport-with-students

WebMD. (n.d.). *Video about the brain on ADHD.* WebMD. https://www.webmd.com/add-adhd/video/brain-adhd

Werb, E. (2021, October 21). *Universal design for learning: 5 strategies that benefit neurodiverse students.* Additude Mag. https://www.additudemag.com/universal-design-for-learning-strategies-adhd/

Wexelblatt, R. (2024, February 9). *Executive function delays in children with ADHD.* Additude Mag. https://www.additudemag.com/executive-function-adhd-kids-lagging-skills/#:~:text=A%20child%20with%20ADHD%20has

What are the most effective ways to engage parents of children with ADHD in their education? (n.d.). LinkedIn. https://www.linkedin.com/advice/0/what-most-effective-ways-engage-parents-children-adhd

Whateley, A. (2022, April 15). *ADHD quotes about the neurodivergent way of paying attention*. Everyday Power. https://everydaypower.com/adhd-quotes/

Willis, A. (n.d.). *Classroom comfort: The role of environmental factors in supporting ADHD students*. MaeToday. https://www.maetoday.org/new-from-mae/classroom-comfort-role-environmental-factors-supporting-adhd-students

Woodward, K. (2023, October 18). *There's no "I" in team: How to work with parents to support students with ADHD*. Pearson Assessments. https://www.pearsonassessments.com/professional-assessments/blog-webinars/blog/2023/10/how-to-work-with-parents-to-support-students-with-adhd.html

Image References

Chernaya, K. (2021). Children with her students holding different color bells [Image]. In *Pexels*. https://www.pexels.com/photo/children-with-her-students-holding-different-color-bells-8535230/

Danilyuk, P. (2021a). Students sitting by their desks inside the classroom [Image]. In *Pexels*. https://www.pexels.com/photo/students-sitting-by-their-desks-inside-the-classroom-8423013/

Danilyuk, P. (2021b). Teachers with their pupils in a classroom [Image]. In *Pexels*. https://www.pexels.com/photo/teachers-with-their-pupils-in-a-classroom-8422126/

Fischer, M. (2020a). A two girls doing peace sign [Image]. In *Pexels*. https://www.pexels.com/photo/a-two-girls-doing-peace-sign-5212662/

Fischer, M. (2020b). Group of students with their teacher [Image]. In *Pexels*. https://www.pexels.com/photo/group-of-students-with-their-teacher-5212352/

Fischer, M. (2020c). Teacher asking a question to the class [Image]. In *Pexels*. https://www.pexels.com/photo/teacher-asking-a-question-to-the-class-5212345/

Grabowska, K. (2020). Portrait of a young woman in eyeglasses in front of a blackboard using smartphone [Image]. In *Pexels*. https://www.pexels.com/photo/portrait-of-a-young-woman-in-eyeglasses-in-front-of-a-blackboard-using-smartphone-6256196/

Krukau, Y. (2021a). A man and children smiling together [Image]. In *Pexels*. https://www.pexels.com/photo/a-man-and-children-smiling-together-8617834/

Krukau, Y. (2021b). Children showing love for their teacher [Image]. In *Pexels*. https://www.pexels.com/photo/children-showing-love-for-their-teacher-8613057/

Loring, V. (2021). Young children doing robotics together [Image]. In *Pexels*. https://www.pexels.com/photo/young-children-doing-robotics-together-7868889/

Mortenson, N. (2021a). Children playing rock paper scissors game [Image]. In *Pexels*. https://www.pexels.com/photo/children-playing-rock-paper-scissors-game-8456139/

Mortenson, N. (2021b). Students sitting on stairs [Image]. In *Pexels*.
https://www.pexels.com/photo/students-sitting-on-stairs-
8457301/

Nilov, M. (2021). Teacher and her student sitting at the table [Image].
In *Pexels*. https://www.pexels.com/photo/teacher-and-her-
student-sitting-at-the-table-8923039/

RDNE Stock Project. (2021a). Smiling boy holding a colored pencil
[Image]. In *Pexels*. https://www.pexels.com/photo/smiling-
boy-holding-a-colored-pencil-8364052/

RDNE Stock Project. (2021b). Woman sitting beside children inside
the classroom [Image]. In *Pexels*.
https://www.pexels.com/photo/woman-sitting-beside-
children-inside-the-classroom-8364069/

Samkov, I. (2020). Students in the classroom [Image]. In *Pexels*.
https://www.pexels.com/photo/students-in-the-classroom-
5676741/

Samkov, I. (2023). Group of people studying together [Image]. In
Pexels. https://www.pexels.com/photo/group-of-people-
studying-together-5676744/

Printed in Great Britain
by Amazon